W9-BMF-547

MANAGING THE CHANGE PROCESS

MANAGING THE CHANGE PROCESS

A Field Book for Change Agents, Consultants, Team Leaders, and Reengineering Managers

David K. Carr

Kelvin J. Hard

William J. Trahant

McGraw-Hill
New York   San Francisco   Washington, D.C.   Auckland   Bogotá
Caracas   Lisbon   London   Madrid   Mexico City   Milan
Montreal   New Delhi   San Juan   Singapore
Sydney   Tokyo   Toronto

Library of Congress Cataloging-in-Publication Data

Carr, David K.
  Managing the change process : a field book for change agents,
consultants, team leaders, and reengineering managers / David K.
Carr, Kelvin J. Hard, William, J. Trahant.
        p.   cm.
  Includes index.
  ISBN 0-07-012944-4 (hardcover : acid-free paper)
  1. Organizational change—Management.   2. Reengineering
(Management)   I. Hard, Kelvin J.   II. Trahant, William J.
III. Title.
HD58.8.C36323   1996
658.4'06—dc20   95-36992
                                                        CIP

McGraw-Hill

A Division of The McGraw-Hill Companies

  3 4 5 6 7 8 9 0   BKP/BKP   9 0 0 9 8

ISBN 0-07-012944-4

*The sponsoring editor for this book was Philip Ruppel, the editing
supervisor was Stephen M. Smith, and the production supervisor was
Pamela A. Pelton. It was set in Fairfield by Terry Leaden of McGraw-
Hill's Professional Book Group composition unit.*

Printed and bound by Quebecor/Book Press.

McGraw-Hill books are available at special quantity discounts to use
as premiums and sales promotions, or for use in corporate training
programs. For more information, please write to the Director of
Special Sales, McGraw-Hill, 11 West 19th Street, New York, NY
10011. Or contact your local bookstore.

 This book is printed on recycled, acid-free paper containing a
minimum of 50% recycled, de-inked fiber.

CONTENTS

FOREWORD

Change is not what it used to be. The status quo will no longer be the best way forward. The best way will be less comfortable and less easy, but, no doubt, more interesting—a word we often use to signal a mix of danger and uncertainty.

CHARLES HANDY, THE AGE OF UNREASON

Change. It has become the one certainty in business today. Mergers, acquisitions, downsizings, and corporate restructurings continue to transform the American business landscape. At the same time, emerging new technologies, the push toward a global economy, and the imperative of all organizations to compete more effectively are all rewriting the rules of business engagement, altering the components of the "psychological" contract that has long existed between employers and employees, and transforming the very nature and notion of work itself.

In the midst of so much change, what can a company or organization do to effectively compete (on a sustained basis) in today's marketplace? How can it develop strategic competitive advantage and continuously reposition itself for success in a constantly changing business environment?

In a word, companies must learn how to manage and *sustain* change in their organizations as part of a continuous process of improvement, renewal, and transformation.

But, as more than a few business writers have noted, many companies today don't do this. Instead, they take a short-term, next-quarter approach to managing their profits and bottom lines. These are the companies that downsize and restructure, for example, expecting that the simple act of cutting costs will increase productivity. Yet we are increasingly aware that bringing about organizational change in this way does not bring the lasting, long-term results we desire. Indeed, downsizing is in some ways the corporate equivalent of a diet. It may reduce the amount of fat we carry for awhile, but by itself it doesn't reenergize or revitalize an organization or give it greater strength and stamina. Downsizing, in fact, frequently cuts into the "muscle" of organizations, resulting in reduced morale and productivity, in lost "competencies" (when highly prized employees leave of their own accord), and in a diminished capacity to compete effectively in the marketplace.

Other companies deal with change in equally ineffective ways. In many cases, they don't act, but simply *react* to the business environment around them. Many of the corporate moves and maneuvers taking place in the marketplace these days are fueled more by a fear of the future than by a clear vision of how to get there—profitably and through sustained growth, suggests *Newsweek*'s Wall Street editor Allan Sloan in the June 19, 1995 issue of the magazine.

Writing, as he does in this case, about the merger frenzy in the high-tech world, and evoking memories of companies like Wang and Digital Equipment, Multimate and Wordstar, Sloan persuasively argues that many high-tech firms today are so haunted by the spector of fear, failure, and being left out of the computer game (as Wang was when it failed to jump on the PC bandwagon) that they resort to desperation moves on the playing field. Ruminating on IBM's bid to buy Lotus, for example, Sloan observes that some companies simply buy up or buy out their competition in an effort to acquire its technology, without considering the sorry history of most corporate takeovers and without subscribing to any longer-term and larger-scale corporate strategy of where they want to go in the future.

Is buying up your competitor's technology or foreclosing on another company's future the way to ensure your own company's lasting market share? Can you capture the essence of another company's business success simply by the stock price you offer for it on Wall Street? I don't believe so, any more than I believe downsizing is a genuine panacea for productivity problems.

Growing and managing a successful organization today requires much more than just buying up other companies and their technologies. Business isn't some large-scale, widescreen monopoly game. Nor is true corporate leadership a spectator sport. Growing and sustaining corporate vitality takes more than simply shifting numbers from one side of the balance sheet to the other as part of a tax write-off, or downsizing so much that your company becomes profitable on paper simply because no one's left on the payroll.

To be successful today, a company must learn how to identify and leverage its strategic intellectual assets. It must learn how to renew itself on a continuous basis and cultivate the habits of organizational resilience. It must, in essence, become what the authors of this book refer to as an "improvement-driven" organization.

What exactly is an improvement-driven organization? For starters, it is one characterized by strong visionary leadership, an obsession with customer focus, a commitment to continuous process improvement, and the *alignment* of both people and processes behind organizational goals and objectives. Improvement-driven organizations are also those that nourish innovation, encourage and foster extensive cross-level and cross-functional communication, and institutionalize the critical importance of change and workplace learning as organizational values.

In my experience, organizations that focus on these key areas of business "competence" are destined for success in today's constantly changing business climate. Such focus is a strong predictor, in fact, of future organizational success, corporate resilience, and sustained business vitality because it forms the basis of long-term competitive advantage in the marketplace.

Moreover, it makes possible a higher-order organizational characteristic that Hamel and Prahalad refer to as "strategic intent."* Simply defined, strategic intent refers to a company's

---

*Gary Hamel and C. K. Prahalad, *Competing for the Future* (Boston: Harvard Business School Press, 1994).

ability to think in the very long-term, to "stretch" and accommodate the changing needs of customers and the shifting demands of the marketplace (without necessarily knowing in that moment perhaps how it's going to get there). Strategic intent refers as well to an organization's ability to leverage its core competencies (its intellectual assets) to gain and *retain* strategic marketplace advantage over time, to position for entry into *new* markets, and to potentially compete on a going-forward basis in several products and/or market arenas.

A company can't easily mimic strategic intent. Nor is it an inborn organizational characteristic. But a company (or organization) can cultivate this trait if it becomes consciously focused on managing change, and internally "harmonized" in ways that allow for the vital interplay of key skills and competencies—specifically, the skills and competencies of its people.

It is when a company begins to experience an internal harmonization of skills and competencies that it begins to operate at peak efficiency and can gain strategic advantage in different products or markets. By reharmonizing over time, it can stay tuned to the needs of its customers and to the shifting demands of a changing marketplace.

But for a company to become organizationally harmonized in this way requires ongoing diligence and "intentionality." It does not occur by accident. It is instead the result of applied and sustained effort on the part of a company's leaders and employees to achieve continuous organizational excellence. And that's why this book, *Managing the Change Process: A Field Book for Change Agents, Consultants, Team Leaders, and Reengineering Managers*, is such an important addition to today's business literature on change management.

In this insightful book, authors David Carr, Kelvin Hard, and William Trahant provide a powerful compass and roadmap with which you and your organization can successfully manage and sustain the change process—principally by becoming aware of and developing best practices in the areas of leadership, customer focus, employee involvement, continuous process improvement, innovation, improvement measurement, and management of change. Moreover, the authors show you how to harness and link the power and *alignment* of people and processes to drive and sustain change within your organization over time.

Drawing on many client case studies and their own wealth of consultative experience, the authors describe how an organization's ability and willingness to implement and sustain change efforts in fact becomes the linchpin on which all future organizational success and effectiveness hinges. They focus on the importance of an organization's fostering and capturing the lessons of new learning and further suggest that what it took for your organization to be succsessful in the past may very well not be a determinant of its success in the future, and could in fact be an obstacle or hindrance to getting there.

Many corporate change books (too many in fact) dwell on the ways in which work processes must be changed or on how costs must be contained to bring about successful organizational transformation. What makes this book different is that it focuses in large part on the interconnections, the "crosswalks" if you will, that must be established and nurtured within an organization, between its people and processes, and among its leaders, managers, and employees if in fact internal harmonization is to result and change at both the *transformational* level (the level of leadership) and the *transactional* level (the level at which day-to-day business is conducted) is to occur.

As a recent Coopers & Lybrand survey pointed out, while executive leadership is the single biggest determinant of whether an organization is high-performing, *equally* important is the understanding that individual employees have of their roles and functions in making change and organizational renewal happen. As the authors note in the Preface that follows, "This is a book about change—the process of aligning people, resources, and culture with a shift in organizational direction."

David Carr, Kelvin Hard, and William Trahant are among the preeminent "thought leaders" in the areas of organizational change, transformational leadership, and change management in the United States today. By combining their knowledge and experience from across a wide variety of fields and industries, they have assembled in this book a critical set of issues for you to examine as you plan change in your organization. By reading this book, you will be able to assess the "change readiness" of your own organization, construct change initiatives according to your business needs, and put strategies and plans in place to make sure that those initiatives are successfully implemented and sustained over time.

This book is not only a primer on how to effectively manage change in your organization, but a continuing reference guide you can use to successfully orchestrate and manage change on an ongoing basis. By reading it, you will gain valuable insight not only into how to achieve short-term improvements in organizational effectiveness and productivity but into how to bring about systemic changes in your organization that will assure long-term growth, profit, and organizational vitality.

Vijay Govindarajan
Earl C. Daum 1924 Professor of International Business
Amos Tuck School of Business Administration
Dartmouth College

PREFACE

This is a book about change—the process of aligning people, resources, and culture with a shift in organizational direction. As a matter of importance to people who participate in the leadership and management of organizations, change may well be the most widely publicized issue in current management literature. Executives, managers, consultants, academics, and journalists thirst for insights into the process of change and its effect on them and their organizations.

We wrote this book to share our insights and to contribute to the dialogue. Our views are informed by our experience with clients, our interaction with colleagues in the field, our survey research into best practices, and the insights we have derived from helping leaders introduce and sustain change in their enterprises.

The domain of the change process encompasses fundamental but far-reaching dimensions that affect an organization's ability to survive and thrive in an economy and marketplace where change is the only predictable constant. In this dynamic environment, leaders are moving away from the "command and control" philosophy to a "lead, coach, and counsel" framework. The transition is not easy, nor even possible, for all of us. It requires a clear vision, an appreciation of behavioral challenges, an understanding of the difference between process and function, a riveting focus on the target, and a conviction that new heights of performance are possible.

Without a vision of the result the change is to produce—and lacking the overt and unrelenting commitment of leaders in the organization—change initiatives do more than fail. Often, they cause additional and unanticipated problems, confronting people with insurmountable challenges. Without vision and leadership, change initiatives are treated as projects of limited duration and value, when they should be part of an ongoing strategy. This strategy's goal is to create a resilient organization capable of constant and positive organizational change in response to a constantly changing environment.

Coopers & Lybrand's recent research confirms the criticality of vision and leadership. As this book goes to press, our Center of Excellence for Change Management is analyzing the results of a best practices survey of 272 high-performance organizations, including *Fortune* 500 companies, major Canadian firms, and large government agencies. Of 65 variables studied, *the chief executive officer's (CEO's) vision was the strongest driving force in achieving measurable results in quality management.* And, according to our study, *these results were the driving force behind high levels of customer satisfaction.*

Still, more than just the CEO must be engaged in the change process. Few would disagree that organizational change is about people—managers, employees, suppliers, and customers—and their capacity to accommodate new ways of behaving and getting work done. Yet many organizations launch change initiatives focused only on "clinical and controllable" technical variables that seem easy to manipulate. We and our clients have learned that focusing on only one set of variables will lead to greatly diminished results.

Our survey makes this abundantly clear. It shows that among the elements leading to high levels of customer satisfaction, innovation, and leading-edge technology are people and management factors. Employees must understand the compelling need for change, and they need to see that their innovative ideas for improvement are readily accepted. Consciously managing change itself predicts success: setting realistic expectations for an organization's ability to change, introducing change at a pace that the organization can assimilate, and ensuring that change leaders have a strong internal base of support.

Unfortunately, we completed the survey too late to incorporate its results into the text of this book, and so must report the initial analyses separately in Appendix C. However, you will find that the text's approach to change management addresses every issue raised in our study. In particular, you will see why organizations that launch major improvement efforts—systems conversions, restructuring, activity-based costing, business process reengineering—without concurrently managing the human dimensions of the change process invariably have marginal or negative outcomes.

For us, this book is part of a continuing effort to learn and share. We believe that the process of change is challenging for all of us. Therefore, contributions to the dialogue about change are both an opportunity and a professional responsibility. We hope our efforts contribute positively to your thinking and stimulate your further contributions to our mutual understanding of the process of change.

David K. Carr
Kelvin J. Hard
William J. Trahant

ACKNOWLEDGMENTS

Coopers & Lybrand, L.L.P. is deeply grateful to those organizations that and persons who, directly through interviews or indirectly through their work with us, made it possible to publish this book. The organizations that participated include ABB Distribution, AlliedSignal, Bell Atlantic, Comalco, The Conference Board, Corsair Marine, Craig Eric Schneier Associates, GTE Telephone Operations, Orange County (Fla.) Corrections Division, PHH Vehicle Management Service, Prudential Direct, Rother & Company, Salomon Brothers, Inc., Southwestern Power Administration, and Tellabs.

Numerous individuals outside our organization made significant contributions to our thinking and understanding. They include William Adler, David Allen, Tom Allison, Lynn Berberich, W. Warner Burke, Mike Codd, Daryl R. Conner, Michel de Rosen, Jean Doyéré, John Gamba, G. Lee Griffin, Paul Hebert, Doug Nelson, Justin O'Connell, Mike Rother, Craig Schneier, Marc Sternfeld, and Jean Taylor.

A number of colleagues within our firm were extremely generous in giving us the benefit of their insights and experience in the change management arena. They include Jim Clark, Roger Cooke, Ian Littman, Wood Parker, Susan Tarkenton, and Kevin Walker. Other in-house staff who offered invaluable support include Don Stoufer, Steve Clyburn, Karen Portman, Jacqui Redmond, and Mike Clover.

We also want to acknowledge the superb research and editorial assistance of Mellen Candage, Saideh Pakravan, Christian Haupt, Margot Fromer, Joy Mara, and Mitchell Dale.

Last but not least, we want to recognize the guidance and direction provided by the members of Coopers & Lybrand's International Change Management Group, especially Michael

Applin (Toronto, Ontario), Peter van der Voorden (Utrecht, Holland), and Hugh Watson (Canberra, Australia).

INTRODUCTION

Outside Acapulco, at La Quebrada, the sea enclosed between jagged cliffs forms a rocky cove that from above appears the size of a handkerchief. Divers thrill visitors by plunging spectacularly from the top of the cliff to the cove 120 feet below. They have to time their dives with the surge of a large wave; otherwise, the water will be too shallow. An untrained person foolhardy enough to dive would no doubt meet a sad fate. But chances are that the highly professional divers, trained in body and in mind, ready for an unexpected shift in parameters such as a gust of wind, a sudden blinding ray of sunlight, or unexpectedly lowered visibility, will achieve a perfect dive.

Business leaders today know that they have to be prepared to take their organizations through change in order to make them leaner and more competitive, but they are also aware that they cannot be like the divers of La Quebrada, perfectly prepared. Even if they could be, the chances of success are not absolute. Too many variables, from the human factor to the emergence of new players, make the game much tougher than it used to be.

Formerly, in the business world as in the wider one, people could operate according to certain laws and principles, the main one being that certain causes would produce certain effects. A company that functioned in a healthy manner and according to sound management practices would earn and keep its share of the market; a product developed and market-ed with care would find customers. But that was a golden age. Today, the relation between cause and effect has shifted, leaving industry leaders worried about the future and a pared down work force in disarray.

However, organizations, like human beings, can grow stronger through setbacks, wiser through experience, and less fragile through adaptability. Another principle that has ruled the earth since it began is survival of the fittest. What that really implies is survival of the adaptable, of the changeable, of the resilient. There are now more shifts and uncertainties in our private, work, and global environment than ever before. By the same token, there are more possibilities for learning to go through change unbroken.

Remember the story of the oak and the reed that both bat-tled a hurricane? The oak thought that, by virtue of its height, sturdiness, and width of trunk, it could weather the elements. The reed, lashed at by furious winds, concentrated on bending in such a manner that it would not break. Guess what? The oak fell, and the reed is still standing.

All organizations today are going through change, on their own initiative or because of compelling needs. Luckily, they can call on management methods and practices that have changed dramatically over the last decades, so that today there is no process that cannot be improved and no issue that can-not be addressed, given the right attitude and the right tools. Because leadership styles and organizational cultures are dif-ferent, there is no universal framework within which every change situation can find a solution. To succeed, a wise com-pany needs to have a blueprint for change adapted to its spe-cific needs. The type of intervention also needs to be suited to the temperament of the individual leader, who can then be a better change sponsor. However, change management can be applied and positive outcomes achieved at almost any stage of an organization's transition from the present state to the desired one.

Throughout its long experience, Coopers & Lybrand has been asked to give expert advice to a wide array of clients in different circumstances, and has developed and honed change management methods that can be applied to fit any change needs, whether in the private or the public sector. This book draws upon our experience. In the course of writing it, we have interviewed change leaders, with many of whom we have had a close working relationship. In in-depth interviews, we have asked them about the changes their organizations have gone through, the difficulties and pitfalls they have faced, the solutions they have found, and the successes they have enjoyed as a result.

We have attempted to put change management in perspective, not as outsiders, but by using real, concrete examples culled from the interviews and from our own long-standing personal involvement. The resulting picture, we hope, accurately portrays the challenges organizations face today and demonstrates how dealing with these challenges through change management can help businesses, not only in America but around the world, adapt to redefined markets.

The first part of this book examines the various components that make up the present business environment, including an overview of breakthrough technologies, management philosophies, the human factor, and the change leader's role. The second part describes the comprehensive Coopers & Lybrand change management methodology and how its organizational models, as well as its tools and techniques, can be adapted to different situations.

Washington Irving once wrote that "there is a certain relief in change, even though it be from bad to worse, as I have found traveling in a stagecoach, that it is often a comfort to shift one's position and be bruised in a new place." For organizations, shock absorbers and a good road map can help make the traveling more comfortable and the destination more rewarding.

CHANGE AND CHANGE MANAGEMENT

HOW ORGANIZATIONS ARE CHANGING

All great changes are irksome to the human mind, especially those which are attended with great dangers and uncertain effects.
JOHN ADAMS

THE GREAT EXPERIMENT

John Adams wrote these words a year after the "shot heard round the world" at the Battle of Concord, Massachusetts, the spark that lit the fuse of the American Revolution. In less than three months, he would sign the Declaration of Independence as a delegate to the Second Continental Congress. During that hot summer in Philadelphia, the future second president of the United States was in the crucible of change, what has been called one of the greatest experiments in human history.

Today, organizations big and small, public and private, domestic and global, are engaged in another great experiment. They find themselves in an era of paradigm shift when a set of assumptions no longer applies and must be replaced. The recent remapping of the world, the emergence of new players on the global scene, and the explosion of technology have created new circumstances to which organizations are learning to adapt. They are responding by adopting new management philosophies and following new methodologies in order to bring about organizational change.

Organizational change means moving from an old way of doing things to a new one that will bring positive outcomes. The transitional stage may be difficult, even painful. Accord-

3

Exhibit 1.1

TELLABS: BUILDING IN CHANGE MECHANISMS

Tellabs, a voice and data transmission equipment manufacturer headquartered in Lisle, Illinois, has always encouraged and fostered change, a vision that permeates the organization. Since its inception in 1975, the company has considered change management not as a buzzword, or the latest fad, or a program, but as a permanent way of doing business, of meeting customer requirements and improving processes. "In fact," says Dan Stolle, the director of human resources, "the hiring strategy calls for looking for people who are always challenging the way things are, even outside their own functional area. The culture encourages this attitude."

Not many organizations have built-in change mechanisms, but most realize that successful change addresses both structures and individuals. It looks beyond development, innovation, or new technology, and usually involves a fundamental redesigning of the structures, accompanied by realignment of the people.

---

ing to consultant and Columbia University Professor W. Warner Burke, "An important part of this change management lies in recognizing and accepting the disorganization and temporary lowered effectiveness that characterize the transition state." Both management commitment and employee support are critical to the success of the desired change.

Any change, but especially major change, disrupts the work environment. In order for an organization and the individuals composing it to continue to function during the disruption, it is essential to plan the change carefully and to align the three elements that make up an organization: the product or service, the human factor, and the culture. Looking beyond the actual transition stage, industry leaders today are also aware that change and its management are not a simple, one-time process but a permanent upheaval to which corporations can adapt only by keeping open and in a permanent learning mode. (See Exhibit 1.1.)

LOGICAL INCREMENTALISM[1]

Since the 1980s, the concept that change can be gradual and incremental has given way to more radical ways of thinking. With the introduction of total quality management (TQM) and continuous improvement, attention to change and change management has acquired scope and immediacy, bringing about a notion of total redesign often expressed in such terms as *transformation, reengineering, rearchitecting,* or *business process redesign (BPR)*. The operative word in business process redesign is *redesign:* to change a business process from stem to stern so that it delivers the strongest possible competitive advantage. However, the days of magic wands are past, and an organization does not change overnight. What happens in practice is that a multitude of small-scale varia-tions and departures from the norm, of small innovations and changes, often called microchanges, interact to build a bigger picture. On the basis of these microchanges, entrepreneurial leaders—i.e., those who know how to be open and alert to new needs—can develop a vision, and thence a strategy, and enter the realm of major, or macrochange. In her book *The Change Masters,* Rosabeth Moss Kanter writes:

> Breakthrough changes that help a company attain a higher level of performance are likely to reflect the interplay of a number of smaller changes that together provide the build-ing blocks for the new construction. Even when attributed to a single dramatic event or a single dramatic decision,

1. James Brian Quinn, *Strategies for Change: Logical Incrementalism* (Homewood, Ill.: Richard D. Irwin, 1980).

major changes in large organizations are more likely to represent the accumulation of accomplishments and tendencies built up slowly over time and implemented cautiously.[2]

EVOLUTION IN ATTITUDE TOWARD CHANGE

A look at the new management philosophies at work in major U.S. corporations shows that an evolution in attitude toward change has occurred in two major areas:

1. *Change is no longer restricted to companies losing money or suffering from obsolete structures.*   A perfectly healthy, profit-making company can often be at the vanguard of introducing change. Here is how Jack Welch, CEO of General Electric, explains his efforts to constantly upgrade the way his organization functions: "You can't simply maintain the status quo, because somebody's always coming from another country with another product, or consumer tastes change, or the cost structure does, or there's a technology breakthrough. If you're not fast and adaptable, you're vulnerable. This is true for every segment of every business in every country in the world."[3]

2. *Business process redesign or the total reengineering of core business processes is a reality.*   A recent article in *Fortune* describes the best corporate candidates for BPR as companies facing big shifts in the nature of competition, particularly in the financial services and telecommunications sector.[4] However, given the magnitude of the paradigm shift, all organizations, whether public or private, face the need to change and adapt to some degree.

2. Rosabeth Moss Kanter, *The Change Masters: Innovation and Entrepreneurship in the American Corporation* (New York: Touchstone, 1984).

3. Stratford Sherman, "A Master Class in Radical Change," *Fortune* (December 13, 1993), pp. 82–90.

4. Thomas Stewart, "Reengineering: The Hot New Managing Tool," *Fortune* (August 23, 1993), pp. 41–48.

CORE CHANGES IN ORGANIZATIONS

New Products

Whether for manufactured goods or for services, customers today can choose from a wide range of options. No longer taken in by slick advertising, the savvy customer needs value. Industries are learning to develop state-of-the-art, high-quality products by attributing high budgets to R&D, using survey tools on customer profile evolution data, and relying increasingly on customer feedback.

A model case is Thermos, where Monte Peterson, who took over as CEO in 1990, soon realized that to be truly competitive in the gas and electric cookout grills market, the company had to come up with a new product. Peterson already knew that "the marketplace is experiencing a revolution as extraordinary as the one inspired by Henry Ford's mass production."[5] Conventional thinking does not take you very far in the present environment; Peterson had already replaced the traditional, function-oriented structure of the company with flexible, cross-functional teams with a rotating leadership depending on the task—an R&D person for technical development, a marketing person for field research, etc. He asked one of these fast-moving teams to develop a new product and then put the team in charge of the project from beginning to end. By defining the market, understanding its needs, and drawing on the company's core competency of vacuum technology, the team developed the Thermal Electric Grill that is now a runaway success. (See Exhibit 1.2.)

Building Core Competencies

Product and quality are important to a company's competitiveness, but building core competencies weighs more in the long run. Core competencies are the collective learning of an orga-

---

5. Brian Dumaine, "Payoff from the New Management," *Fortune* (December 13, 1993), pp. 103–110.

Exhibit 1.2

THERMOS'S THERMAL ELECTRIC GRILL

nization, whether in products or in services. To ensure these, a company must work across functional boundaries to ensure good communication on market needs and technological possibilities. Sony's capacity to miniaturize, Philips's optical-media know-how, or Citicorp's operating system that allows it to participate in world markets 24 hours a day are some examples of core competencies. Casio's expertise in display systems and Honda's in engines are others. Honda's engines are core products, which also means that the design and development skills that go into them lead to a proliferation of end products. "It is essential to make this distinction between core competencies, core products, and end products, because global competition is played out by different rules and for different stakes at each level."[6] Building around a handful of core competencies and core products is one way of establishing world leadership. In the mid-1970s, when JVC established videocassette recorder (VCR) supply relationships with leading national consumer electronics companies in Europe and the United States, it gathered enough expertise to start establishing its own core products. Asian companies have often established an advantage in the component market and gone on to build brand leadership which, in turn, is often followed by price leadership.

Demographics

The workplace in America is going through convulsions that an article in *Fortune* calls "an historic event, the Western equivalent of the collapse of communism."[7]

The end of the Cold War is highly instrumental in these convulsions, causing major job cuts and a realignment in the defense industry. However, downsizing is not limited to the defense industry. The pressure of competition has forced all companies to deal with work force issues. The trend toward leaner, flatter structures, the intense focus on productivity, and cost control have produced an ongoing downsizing process.

The human factor will be the most affected, because for the first time in the economic history of nations, economic growth will not mean full employment but a continuous downsizing of the labor force. Even recovery will not create jobs. When *Inc.* magazine recently published its list of fastest-growing companies, it added the following data: Although the combined sales of the 100 firms on the list increased 18-fold from 1988 to 1993, the number of employees increased only six-fold.[8]

6. C. K. Prahalad and Gary Hamel, "Core Competence," *Harvard Business Review* (May/June 1990), pp. 79–91.

7. Stratford Sherman, "How Will We Live with the Tumult?" *Fortune* (December 13, 1993), pp. 123–125.

8. Steven Pearlstein, "Fleet-Footed Firms Reshape Economy," *The Washington Post* (July 4, 1994), pp. A1, A8.

Along with cutting staff, companies are constantly speeding up production. More union organizing is one result. In the meat packing industry, where speed has more than doubled in recent years, unions are voicing their concerns for safety. At a General Motors plant in Shreveport, Louisiana, a plan to speed up the assembly line while reducing personnel recently met with strong resistance. Layoffs, downsizing, and safety problems cause the work force to react negatively to what it often perceives as a bleak future. Only industry managers able to manage the pain of taking their organization from the generous corporate structure of the last decades to the meaner, leaner present one can hope to remain competitive.

INFORMATION TECHNOLOGY

- Real estate agencies install locks on the doors of properties for sale, which agents activate when showing the property to a potential customer. A computer then registers arrival and departure times and how much time was spent visiting the property. It also keeps track of how often the property was shown during a given period, the average time this property and similar ones remain on the market, etc.
- At UPS, packages are bar-coded, allowing scanning at each delivery point. Package tracing permits the company to pinpoint packages for customers and eliminate troublesome paperwork and time cards.[9]
- In businesses with field staff, salespeople input customer orders directly into their laptop computers, so that orders are filled correctly with fewer processing steps.

These are three examples of the versatile, all-encompassing use of information technology that has literally revolutionized the business world. And yet, according to communications experts, information technology is still in its earliest

---

9. Robert Frank, "Driving Harder," *The Wall Street Journal* (May 23, 1994), p. A1.

stages. In a report commissioned by Coopers & Lybrand, G2 Research Inc. showed that in 1992 U.S. organizations would spend nearly $18 billion reengineering their information systems, an investment increasing to $40 billion by 1997, with the lion's share going for: new hardware; converting old computer codes into newer, more powerful and flexible languages; and ensuring better communication among different hardware configurations. When properly used, information technology is a powerful tool for increasing speed, quality, and flexibility, and for creating new, different, and effective process operations. It enables businesses to maximize their return on investment and deliver breakthroughs in competitive advantage. However, in the past three decades, many organizations have only been paving cow paths, sending millions of dollars down the drain by applying sophisticated information technology to automate existing processes. The consequence? Making the same mistakes faster. Firms are catching on, though, and learning to synchronize technology and processes. Information technology is a key facilitating device for new designs, whether at the organizational or work process level. Says consultant David Nadler, "Information systems, common architectures, shared databases, decision support tools, and expert systems facilitate the coordination of autonomous units linked together through information."[10]

NEW MANAGEMENT METHODOLOGIES AND PHILOSOPHIES

In the corporate world today, archaic and traditional structures are history. Agility and flexibility are the new key concepts. Business leaders envision reconfigurable designs that can change almost on demand. New managers learn and use techniques and management policies disseminated by gurus and consultants. The names of these new tools vary, but whatever the method, the focus is on speeding up processes and

10. David Nadler and Mark S. Gerstein, *Organizational Architecture* (New York: Jossey Bass, 1992).

improving work flow and output. They all aim toward lean productivity, cost reduction, breakthrough in product development, global competition. In other words, they are about making change happen.

BUSINESS PROCESS REDESIGN

A fundamental rethinking and redesign of business processes to achieve dramatic improvements in critical measures of performance such as cost, quality, service, and speed, business process redesign (BPR) is one term used to describe how organizations achieve radical improvement over a short period. BPR is neither casual nor easy. Beyond vision and commitment, it requires a comprehensive approach to change that includes external orientation in analyzing processes (based on customer research, competitive and economic analysis, and benchmarking), the use of information technology, a sound change strategy, and effective change management. Proven technologies that support business process reengineering—such as cycle time analysis, for instance—have demonstrated their own value. (See Exhibit 1.3.)

Exhibit 1.3

BPR: THE BREAKTHROUGH-MAKER

CONTINUOUS INCREMENTAL IMPROVEMENT PROVIDES SMALL, ONGOING CHANGE	BUSINESS PROCESS REDESIGN CREATES RAPID, REVOLUTIONARY CHANGE
Current processes are reasonably close to customer requirements	Existing processes incapable of meeting current customer or competitor requirements
Accepts the status quo as the basis for improvement	Challenges the fundamentals
Uses technology incrementally	Views technology as a process transformer
Involves less risk because impact is usually narrow	Involves more risk because impact is large, cross-cutting
Cost of making change is usually small, often "free"	Cost of making change is often very large

Outsourcing

Part of the BPR philosophy is outsourcing, which allows companies to limit themselves strictly to their own core competency and have everything else done outside. Looking beyond in-house capabilities saves money and makes a process more efficient, as suppliers usually use their core competency to come up with appropriate products and become more efficient at performing particular tasks. Suppliers also have to reduce prices and meet high standards or else be dropped, which to small companies, many of which depend on one major customer, can mean the difference between life and death. The chosen partners often receive long-term contracts.

Usually, the partnership is rewarding for both sides, though sometimes, relying too heavily on one customer or one source can be taxing. Chrysler, for instance, is becoming increasingly dependent on Mitsubishi and Hyundai for its engines, which between 1985 and 1987 grew from 252,000 to 382,000 per year. Honda, on the other hand, refuses to yield manufacturing responsibility, much less design, of so critical a part of a car's function as an engine to an outside company. For years, Honda has been committed to Formula One auto racing, so that despite a relatively small R&D budget it could develop very competitive products from its own engine-related technologies, based on its own experience. Honda has now switched to the American Indycars for the same reason.

To outsource or not to outsource? There can be advantages to both systems. Producing in-house allows lower coordinating costs—salesmen, advertising, or debt collection—but outside contractors usually come up with the most competitive price.

When they have a choice, companies often choose to contract work to lower-cost outside shops. The decision to outsource sometimes causes uneasiness and anxiety, provoking workers to respond negatively—in June 1994, workers went on strike at General Motors to protest new outside contracts—but the solution is usually advantageous to both parties.

TOTAL QUALITY MANAGEMENT

Management philosophies are not just fads. *BusinessWeek* recently published the results of a test that suggests an impact of TQM on stock value. According to the CEO of Laura Ashley, "Quality has become basic hygiene."[11]

TQM involves management commitment, product quality, continuous improvement, teamwork, and ongoing training, and can be attained by cascading steps: management awareness, strategic planning, management implementation, employee training. Both analytical aspects—tools, procedures, statistics—and process improvement must be addressed. The behavioral aspects monitor how individuals respond in process improvement as well as in their daily work. Leadership must push together and integrate the two aspects into a holistic culture in which employees are equally skilled and supported in both. (See Exhibit 1.4.)

REENGINEERING

TQM can *improve* processes, but in a much acclaimed book published in 1993,[12] Michael Hammer and James Champy advocate starting over, or reengineering, a methodology very similar to BPR. Like BPR, reengineering involves the "fundamental rethinking and radical redesign of business processes to achieve dramatic improvement in critical, contemporary measures of performance, such as cost, quality, service, and speed." It should be limited to carefully selected processes that have a major impact on outside customers, for instance, and whose redesign is feasible in terms of scope and cost. Even then, an estimated 70 to 90 percent of reengineering projects do not significantly improve their operational objectives.[13] Says Michael Hammer, "To succeed in reengineering, you have to be a visionary, a motivator, and a leg breaker."

11. James Maxmin, CEO, Laura Ashley, "Productivity: Key to World Competitiveness," presentation at conference cosponsored by The Conference Board and the Peter F. Drucker Foundation for Nonprofit Management (April 1, 1993).

12. Michael Hammer and James Champy, *Reengineering the Corporation* (New York: Harper Business, 1993).

13. Karen Schwartz, "The Latest Catch-Phrase or a Sea Change?" *Solution Channels* (supplement to *Washington Technology*) (May 19, 1994), pp. S12–S14.

Exhibit 1.4

TQM

TRADITIONAL MANAGEMENT	TOTAL QUALITY MANAGEMENT
Needs of users of products and services defined by specialists	*Customer focus*, in which users of products and services define what they want
Errors and waste tolerated if they do not exceed set standards	*No tolerance* for errors, waste, and work that does not add value to products and services
Products and services inspected for problems, then "fixed"	*Prevention* of problems
Many decisions governed by assumptions and gut feelings	*Fact-based decisions*, using hard data and scientific procedures
Short-term planning based on budget cycle	*Long-term planning*, based on improving mission performance
Product or service designed sequentially by isolated departments	*Simultaneous design* of total product or service life cycle by teams from many functions
Control and improvement by individual managers and specialists	*Teamwork* among managers, specialists, employees, vendors, customers, and partner agencies
Improvement focused on onetime breakthroughs, such as computers and automation	*Continuous improvement* of every aspect of how work is donex
Vertical structure and centralization, based on control	*Horizontal and decentralized structure*, based on maximizing value added to products and services
Short-term contracts awarded, based on price	*Vendor partnership* of long-term buyer/seller obligations, based on quality and continuous improvement

LEAN PRODUCTION

Lean production started as Toyota's answer to the American assembly line that it could not afford to replicate. Also, the Japanese had no wish to import, along with the technical know-how, the problems that plagued U.S. mass production, such as a high number of defective parts, huge inventories, and badly organized human and material resources. The new system, with its highly measurable improvements—reduction of waste, lower inventories, sophisticated benchmarking, and a productivity rate of 20 to 30 percent higher for Japanese workers compared to their European or American counterparts—was soon copied everywhere. Now adopted by the world motor industry, lean production can mean using about half the traditional factory space and about one-tenth the inventories. With faster product development and dramatically improved quality and productivity, lean organizations also find a payoff in lower costs and the ability to bring out different models faster, at higher volume, and with higher quality.

The method does come under heavy criticism, especially from unions, which see it as a means to undermine them. Yet integrating efficiency with quality resembles the principle of constant improvement that the Japanese call *kaizen*, "the never-ending quest for perfection."[14]

JUST-IN-TIME

Lean production depends on such practices as just-in-time (JIT) manufacturing, the cycle time management in which a precise number of parts are delivered to the assembly line right before they are needed. JIT can be a powerful inventory system, but it depends on a supplier/manufacturer relationship based on trust: A small supplier that has to bend over backward to accommodate a client—usually a large corporation—will often ask to be the sole supplier. The manufacturer, on the other hand, needs to be able to call on other sources should the habitual one fail.

CYCLE TIME REDUCTION

Also called time-based management, cycle time reduction (CTR) is an effective way of making sure that actual work is being done during the time spent to make a product. At AlliedSignal, one of the corporations that has made spectacu-

---

14. Tom Peters, *Thriving on Chaos: Handbook for a Management Revolution* (New York: Knopf, 1987), p. 283.

lar use of CTR, managers found that actual work was being done only 10 to 20 percent of the time of the entire process. For instance, it was taking two weeks for a part to go from receiving dock to storeroom—a time reduced now to two hours! Through mapping out each manufacturing process, the details can be worked out, and time-consuming steps, or downtime, such as waiting for work orders to be signed, can be eliminated.

CUSTOMER FOCUS

In his book *Thriving on Chaos,* Tom Peters says that "There is a nearly unanimous opinion forming that in the 1990s we'll be running business primarily by customer-oriented processes."[15] Nowadays, management strategies depend heavily on customer feedback. The objective of all companies is to reach their customers faster than the competition, with a product honed by surveys and focus groups to obtain customer preference and achieve customer satisfaction. At Conrail, the transport of finished autos is one of the more exacting tasks, so the company has taken delivery of this commodity out of its core network and gives it special handling. In the past, says the firm's director of employee services, the attitude was, "We're running a schedule, and if you would like us to move your freight, be here at the right time. Today, we are much more customer-oriented."

Compared to even a few years ago, companies have shifted from being product-oriented or profit-oriented to being customer-oriented. In the words of the GTE leadership, "Always begin with the customer. Customer needs drive everything we do."[16]

Only organizations becoming resolutely customer-oriented can attract customers and create loyalty.

15. Peters, op. cit.

16. David P. Allen, "Dreaming and Doing: Reengineering GTE Telephone Operations," *Planning Review* (March/April 1993), pp. 28–31.

EMPOWERMENT

As organizations delayer their hierarchy, they learn to function in a more focused environment. The necessary corollary is to empower the leaner work force, to organize cross-functional teams in which increased responsibility and accountability become the incentives to better operations. Empowerment is often confused with delegation or the ability of employees to act on their decisions. What it really means is that employees are asked to offer feedback and valuable ideas that management, in turn, listens to and eventually acts upon.

At one General Electric plant, the product had always moved down whether or not a worker was finished. Management changed that by giving employees the responsibility for deciding when to move the product from their station to the next. Here is how CEO Jack Welch describes the result: "People on the assembly line now found two levers in front of them. One lever stopped the line. The other sent a part on its way only after an individual was satisfied that it was perfect. The line workers suddenly became the final authority on the quality of their work. The cynics scoffed when this system was proposed, predicting chaos or production at a snail's pace. What happened? Quality increased enormously and the line ran faster and smoother than ever."[17] (See Chap. 4 for a more detailed discussion on empowerment.)

TEAMWORK

When Paul Hebert, former president of Corsair, a yacht builder, describes his beginnings with the company, this is what he says: "We used to sail every boat before we delivered it. Our people would come back with long lists of things that needed to be fixed. But in the last six months, they started coming back with nothing on their lists—we were doing everything right the first time. One reason for this was we made

---

17. Robert Slater, *The New GE: How Jack Welch Revived an American Institution* (Hamate, Ill.: Business One Irwin, 1993).

each team in the production process responsible for getting their work right before passing it to the next team."

Teams do not just happen; they must be trained and developed. More and more often, they are cross-functional teams that cut across the former silo structures of organizations where each function worked on its own. The trend now is to create teams that contain representatives from various divisions, with a rotating leadership as well as team accountability. (See Chap. 3 for a more detailed discussion on teams.)

NEW ORGANIZATIONAL STRUCTURES

To quote Jack Welch again, the organization of the future will be boundaryless, and to achieve that, "You need to blow up the company's floors and walls." Without going to such extremes, corporations today are rearchitecting their hierarchy to achieve horizontal structures by downsizing middle management and using teams and training all employees. Examples besides General Electric include divisions of AT&T, Eastman Kodak, Motorola, and Xerox.

"Productivity is high. Employees recognize there are fewer layers and fewer opportunities to advance. On the other hand, they are seeing more cross-functional cooperation than ever, and more opportunities to shine, with appropriate awards."[18]

Mammoth corporations are disappearing, fragmented into more flexible units. One implication of flattened organizations is that the command structure flow is different, often lateralized rather than coming from the top, with minimized bureaucracy as corollary. The underlying philosophy is that in smaller, less rigid structures, employees are closer to the customers and can respond faster.

---

18. Bob Marshall and Larry Kelleher, "A Test of Restructuring Success," *HR Magazine* (August 1993), pp. 82–85.

WORK FORCE AND MANAGEMENT RESPONSE TO CHANGE

In an organization ideally adapted to these changing times, management would have not only a clear vision of where it wants to go but a well-thought-out strategy for getting there, and employees would be active and interested fellow travelers. Tom Peters argues for happy, easy change when he says that "The chief job of the leader, at all levels, is to oversee the dismantling of dysfunctional old truths and to prepare people and organizations to deal with—to love, to develop affection for—change per se."[19]

The reality of change does not quite coincide with this idealistic picture. In fact, people resist change more often than not. Organizational development experts often like resistance or negative responses, which they take as signs of vitality; however, organizational leaders who find themselves fighting resistance every step of the way are wasting energy better spent in building the future.

NEGATIVE RESPONSES

By shattering the status quo, change naturally provokes resistance. This is even more the case in a period of economic uncertainty, when any difference in the work environment is perceived by the work force as job-threatening. Even companies that have been working with change management over the last few years have difficulty obtaining employee commitment to organizational and cultural change.

Of his experience with the changes at Xerox, CEO Paul Allaire says: "The hardest stuff is the soft stuff—values, personal style, ways of interacting. We are trying to change the total culture of the company. When you talk about it in gener-

---

19. Peters, op. cit.

al terms, everybody is all for it. But when you talk about it in terms of individuals, it is much tougher. And yet, if individuals don't change, nothing changes."[20]

POSITIVE RESPONSES

Experience shows that the greater employee involvement in the change, the greater the positive response in understanding the compelling need for the change and the sharing of the vision. ASEA Brown Boveri is a star global corporation whose powerful chairman, Percy Barnevik, stresses the importance of asking and winning employee commitment in the change. His method is to ask employees to evaluate new ideas and practices. "We human beings are driven by habit, history, and the rearview mirror. If you want to break direction, you have to shake people up, not by threatening them, not by offering a bonus, but by illustrating in a similar situation what can be accomplished."[21]

Management gurus suggest giving people a sense of safety in learning, in trying new things, without fear of punishment. When failure is not blamed but considered part of the learning process, people feel secure in taking bold steps outside their narrow territory, and that is when things start happening. Communication, ongoing training programs, and surveys that give a general picture of the state of mind of an organization's labor pool at any given time and allow adjustments are all useful adjuncts in making employees feel they have a vested interest in the company's future beyond their personal ones.

HOW INSTITUTIONS HAVE RESPONDED

Despite economic indicators all clearly pointing to the necessity of reacting fast or being left behind, many institutions

---

20. Robert Howard, "The CEO as Organizational Architect: An Interview with Xerox's Paul Allaire," *Harvard Business Review* (September/October 1992), pp. 106–121.

21. Gail E. Schares, "Percy Barnevik's Global Crusade," *BusinessWeek* (special enterprise issue, October 22, 1993), pp. 204–211.

remain risk-averse and prefer to proceed with caution. Others, taken with the new buzzwords and the image of a handful of change leaders, plunge headlong into redesigning or reengineering without taking all factors into consideration. But more and more leaders, in organizations of all sizes, perceive that not only is change imperative to adapt to the current markets, but change strategy and change management need to accompany the transformational movement. Even then, the results are not guaranteed. As Mike Walsh, the late chairman of Tenneco, said in a candid moment, "In my opinion, there are two kinds of businesses in the United States: those that are heading for the cliff and know it, and those that are heading the same way but don't know it. Our advantage is, we know it."[22]

Most of today's organizations fall into one of three broad categories:

1. *Companies that have no conscious change management strategy.* There are still rigid corporations or conservative institutions in the United States that think that their culture, their way of doing things, has served them well and needs no adjustments. But management principles once considered axiomatic are being challenged daily. Even the federal government, not a particularly progressive organization, realizes the need to adapt to the new trends of the market and the new demands of the public.

2. *Companies that take a tactical view or have incomplete strategies.* Many companies decide to overhaul or restructure without first analyzing and articulating both business practices to be changed and the strategy for implementing the change. Overlooking this crucial preparation for change and its implementation too often breeds failure.

3. *Companies that have a clear strategy.* A more enlightened approach to major change involves first analyzing the present situation, then defining the nature and the scope of the

---

22. Stratford Sherman, "A Master Class in Radical Change," *Fortune* (December 13, 1993), pp. 82–90.

change necessary, and finally articulating vision, goal, and strategy while maximizing employee involvement.

MODELS FOR SUCCESSFULLY IMPLEMENTING CHANGE

Conceptual models on the character and process of change share common ideas. The principal is one that change process must derive from the company's natural and established capabilities—in other words, be a good fit.

Successful models have these elements in common:

1. *They address change in a comprehensive manner.*   An example is the Burke-Litwin Model, developed by W. Warner Burke, of Columbia University, and George Litwin, formerly of Harvard. It deals with organizations as systems and classifies the key social behavioral factors that influence performance in an organization. These factors, divided into *transformational* (leadership, organizational culture, mission, and strategy, etc.) and *transactional* (management practices, systems, individual needs, and values, etc.), are organized into causal relationships: affecting one variable means affecting others. In a change management situation, a systems theory approach is useful in determining the sequence in which key factors should be addressed. (See Chap. 7 for further discussion.)

2. *They follow a process for introducing change.*   Coopers & Lybrand uses a four-step model that is not a change master plan but a way of getting started. It seeks to:

- *Assess.*   Analyze the data for an accurate diagnosis of the "as is" situation and create an understanding of the change problems.
- *Plan.*   Articulate and define the tactical change process required to bridge the gap between "as is" and "to be."
- *Implement.*   Support and reinforce commitment.
- *Renew.*   Involve and empower people toward a shared vision and a culture change.

3. *They address a set of critical success factors.*   When organi-

zations set aside assumptions and axioms that no longer work and start looking at structural and cultural elements with an open mind, a whole new set of factors appears. Some of these involve the leadership's ability to create a shared vision, plan the change process, understand the human aspect involved, and build in a capacity for ongoing learning and development. By addressing these factors, not only in the early stages of the change process, but with a constantly challenging attitude, organization leaders can create limitless opportunity for growth.

ORGANIZATIONS CAN BUILD RESILIENCE AND A CAPACITY FOR MAKING CHANGE HAPPEN

Individuals react differently when confronted by unforeseen change and developments that can affect them adversely. Some fall apart; others actually thrive in changing, fluctuating environments. They face the challenge and regain their equilibrium faster. This is what resilience is about: the ability to bounce back faster than others. In an organization undergoing change, building a resilient work force by widely disseminating the change vision and strategy and by minimizing disruption is essential. These steps diminish negative feelings about the change and can save time and money, because they help employees adjust more quickly and maintain performance levels more evenly. The successful introduction of change rests on its *management*, planned but with a flexible, adaptable structure. A consequence of building a resilient work force is that the organization itself develops resilience, too, as well as its own built-in responses to the management of change.

How, then, can change management be summed up?

1. *Change management is a core competency of the improvement-driven organization.* Focusing on core competencies— what the company does best, in terms of product—is important if companies want to reinforce their specialized niche and

project a clear image. But organizations are just now learning they can develop core competencies in change management as well. That can be achieved by building effective teams; by encouraging empowerment, creativity, and learning skills; and by widely disseminating information on strategy and achievement. The higher the comfort level about the organization's culture and environment, the more efficient employees will be at their jobs, and the easier for them to become flexible and take change in stride.

2. *Change management is a critical executive/manager skill.* The list of requisite skills for today's managers can be mind-boggling, and so can a cultural and psychological topology of managers and their approach. Whatever the variables, certain assets are critical. Among them are an analytical mind, leadership ability, a good comfort level in the face of ambiguity, and the ability to build resilience by creating a "listening environment."[23]

3. *Change management is an aspect of becoming a learning organization.* "Learning is no longer a choice but a necessity, and the most urgent priority is learning how to learn faster."[24] When a learning organization provides information and training on a continuous basis, not only for knowledge but for performance, it develops its people skills while promoting a capacity for adaptability and resilience.

"At the heart of a learning organization is a shift of mind—from seeing ourselves as separate from the world to connected to the world, from seeing problems as caused by someone or something 'out there' to seeing how our own actions create the problems we experience. A learning organization is a place where people are continually discovering how they create their reality."[25]

23. Peters, op. cit.

24. Edgar Schein, "How Can Organizations Learn Faster?" *Sloan Management Review* (Winter 1993), pp. 85–92.

25. Peter Senge, *The Fifth Discipline: The Art and Practice of the Learning Organization* (New York: Doubleday Currency, 1990), pp. 12–13.

GLOBAL PERSPECTIVES: PROGRESS AND CHALLENGES IN ORGANIZATIONAL CHANGE MANAGEMENT

What we had were two streams of activities. One we called "breakthrough project," aimed at the changes in the organization's processes; the other was our "let's get our house clean" project, what we called housekeeping.   JEAN DOYÉRÉ, ABB DISTRIBUTION

Organizations talk about remapping when they redesign structures, boundaries, and functions. But remapping is also a reality when applied to today's world, affecting development strategies worldwide. Not even a decade ago, an atlas was a reliable reference. Now, carved-in-stone ideologies that polarized the globe for 70 years have collapsed, changing an entire world order. Massive political, economic, and geographical transformations have taken place. Large and mainly untapped markets are opening in China, India, and the newly independent countries of the former Soviet Union. In 1997, Hong Kong will no longer be a British protectorate but returns to Chinese rule. The spectacular success story of newly industrialized countries (NICs) is another relatively recent development. (In the last 25 years, per capita income in Hong Kong, South Korea, Taiwan, and Singapore has grown more than four times as fast as in the rest of the world.[1]) Well into recession, Japan is no longer a threat to U.S. global economic leadership.

As a result of this transformation, governments for emerging countries aim to establish free-market economies and major companies strive to create an extensive global presence to take advantage of the new possibilities. Most countries are now aligned on the concept of free-market economy. However, economic liberalization in countries that until yesterday functioned according to strictly imposed guidelines does not mean the end of problems. In Europe, decades of socialism have produced welfare programs with rocketing costs as unemployment soars. Expensive labor, the weight of social benefits, and the difficulty of downsizing in heavily unionized industries contribute to make organizations less competitive than in developing countries and the NICs of Asia. Ethnic and political disruption in former Eastern European countries has led to a massive emigration of their citizens to the West.

In the United States, the end of the Cold War has had far-reaching repercussions. The defense sector has been hit particularly hard. Historically a spearhead of innovation, national defense also created a huge pool of skilled, well-paid workers. In 1991, military spending accounted for six million jobs in the U.S. Now, according to the Congressional Office of Technology Assessment, by the year 2001, there will be a loss of 2.5 million jobs in the defense sector, an average of 250,000 a year.[2] In a recent study, *Fortune* magazine estimates that the number of defense suppliers that reached approximately 120,000 under the Reagan Administration has dropped to around 30,000. Under President Clinton, the federal government supports the development of innovative technology with commercial applications, but the conversion will take time.

---

1. A. Peter Petri, "The NICs: Pragmatic Policymakers," *International Economic Insights* (March/April 1993), pp. 2–5.

2. U.S. Congress, Office of Technology Assessment, "After the Cold War: Living with Lower Defense Spending," OTA-ITE524 (Washington, D.C.: Government Printing Office, February 1992).

Over the next five years, overall defense spending will decline to 3.6 percent of gross domestic product (GDP), the lowest level since the 1940s. With this rapid decline, defense firms, used to complex technology, are finding they have to redefine patterns and learn adaptability. As someone recently said, "There is no demand for a stealth refrigerator." Also, accustomed as they are to a captive government market, these firms will have to acquire marketing expertise to convert to commercial business.

All these changes have an enormous impact on corporations worldwide. Companies realize that to remain competitive in such a market, they must make major adjustments. The 1993 Conference Board survey finds that, generally, firms in the United States and their European subsidiaries find it easier than Europe-based firms to make a major change in strategy. On the other hand, European companies are slightly more likely than those in the U.S. to have undergone major structural changes such as delayering (moving away from hierarchical organizations toward flatter ones).

In the same survey, half the participants consider their organizational redesign a success. Out of 160 respondents, 70 percent consider themselves to be a global company with geographic or business units allowed relative freedom. Most carry change initiatives across country borders. Global companies appear to be moving to regionalize the way they operate, though that is not apparent in implementation of change management activities among survey respondents.

A recent survey of American executives found that fewer than half felt their companies were very capable of coping with change; 25 percent could not name *any* company that was good at managing change.[3] Is this pessimism justified? What is driving change in spite of organizational reluctance? Are organizations struggling or succeeding when it comes to making change—and what needs to improve?

---

3. K. Hammonds, "Changing But Not Happy about It," *BusinessWeek* (September 20, 1993).

This chapter provides a snapshot of organizations' experiences with change management in private and public organizations across the continents today. Our discussion is based on review and synthesis of a number of surveys conducted with organizations in Europe, Australia, and North America, many of which are multinational in scope, and on information from Coopers & Lybrand's Organizational Assessment Process database of 400 international companies. Although the organizations, nationalities, and survey topics are diverse, the themes that emerge are remarkably similar. Organizations face common pressures to change, address common change issues and obstacles, and most have taken some (but not always enough or the most effective) action to manage change. They are also coming to recognize that change is not only here to stay; its speed is increasing.

WHY ORGANIZATIONS INITIATE CHANGE: COMMON COMPELLING NEEDS

It is axiomatic that real change succeeds only in the presence of a compelling need for it. Today, four types of forces are driving organizations to change, ready or not:

1. *Market forces.*   These include global competition, new market opportunities, and changing customer needs and preferences. Noel Goutard of France's Valeo, a large vehicle parts maker, sums up the situation his company and others are facing. "I've never seen changes take place without strong incentive. The incentives are here now: erratic markets, Japanese competition, intense job pressure. They are forcing change."[4]

"What are we going to do," asks Jack Welch, CEO of General Electric, "when a restructured and hungry Europe

---

4. P. Hofheinz, "Europe's Tough New Managers," *Fortune* (September 6, 1993), pp. 111–115.

5. Jack Welch, "CEOs on the Economy: A Matter of Exchange Rates," *The Wall Street Journal* (June 21, 1994).

and a lean, low-cost Japan, with improved economies, come roaring back—show them our press clippings?"[5] Welch, urging members of the Economic Club of Detroit not to rely on a weak U.S. dollar to keep American companies competitive, described the international dynamics of today's marketplace, which leave no country room for complacency. Welch also talked about market opportunities that are driving change, stating that "Asia is the greatest growth market we will see in our careers. It is our future."

2. *Rapidly changing technologies.* Technology today changes almost as quickly as the weather, and long-term forecasts have similar reliability. In Europe, after a promising start, information technology, bogged down by high wages and a generous welfare system, has been unable to remain innovative. In the United States, Edward R. McCracken, CEO of Silicon Graphics, says, in his industry cutting-edge innovation is the only real source of competitive advantage. "No one can plan the future," he explains. "Three years is long-term [for strategic planning]. Even two years may be. Five years is laughable."[6] The rapid pace of technological change is also relevant to organizations that use technologies. They offer the potential for competitive advantage or parity, but only when an organization changes to create new ways of doing business using the high-tech tools. The days of gaining lasting advantage from simply automating current processes are over. (See Exhibit 2.1.)

3. *Changing political institutions and societies.* Putting businesses and services in private hands has long been a factor of increased activity and productivity. Over the past decades, European socialist governments, in the first flush of political victory, nationalized or kept nationalized major manufacturing and services industries. But when they realized it was harming the economy, they soon started reversing the policy. In the U.S., deregulation, added to foreign competition, has helped

6. S. Prokesch, "Mastering Chaos at the High-Tech Frontier," *Harvard Business Review* (November/December 1993), pp. 134–144.

Exhibit 2.1

DEVELOPING A GLOBALLY COMPETITIVE PRODUCT

In this redefined world, competition is fierce and only constant improvement can help sustain a competitive advantage. Even for well-established firms, lack of drive eventually spells loss of market share. Michael Porter cites the machine tool industry, where in the space of a decade British and American firms lost almost century-old positions to rivals using new computer technology. Porter discusses German firms who lost their lead in cameras when the Japanese developed single reflex technology. The Japanese in turn gave up a substantial share in shipbuilding when improvement slowed and Korean firms replicated their strategies with cheaper labor.

Various factors intervene in giving companies a global, sustainable, and competitive advantage. Reputation and brand names are a powerful lever. Other advantages can be proprietary process technology, important R&D and marketing budgets, and powerful after-sales service networks. For the time being, American electronics firms cannot be dethroned by Korean ones, no matter how resourceful the latter. However, no leading position remains secure for long, and entire industries can be wiped out if, in the long run, they are unable to compete in one or the other of the activities forming the value chain. Only through constant upgrading of processes and mentality can organizations face the new global challenges and establish a competitive strategy. Market boundaries change fast, and any success is temporary. Major companies find they have to change radically in order to maintain gained territory.

Exhibit 2.1 (*Continued*)

A company's leader must create a context in which widening and upgrading advantage is viewed as normal and expected. For example, the norm should be to move early to address factor cost pressures, rather than passively hoping that government policy will reverse them. In practice, such an orientation toward change is hard to accomplish from within. A leader must create an atmosphere that highlights the need for upgrading and demands that it take place.*

*Michael Porter, *The Competitive Advantage of Nations* (New York: The Free Press, 1990), p. 583.

raise service-sector productivity to a 1.6 percent annual rate in the 1990s, double its 0.8 percent in the 1980s.

The two most significant trends are the privatization of organizations that once were government- or monopoly-run and the need for government organizations to become more efficient and less costly to operate. Mike Codd, former secretary of the Department of the Prime Minister and Cabinet in Australia, describes the scenario the Australian government faced in 1987 (a familiar one to many government organizations today). "[There was] a perception over many years amongst senior people in the government service that the system of large numbers of departments was inefficient, was subject to constant change and disruption, allowed overlapping of responsibilities and boundaries in a way which created tension and territorialism, and was generally not the best way of managing government effectively."

In addition to total government "reinventions," many individual agencies are facing pressures to change. In Orlando, Florida, the Orange County Corrections Division cut its budget by $4 million through improved management systems and employee empowerment. The impetus: "The chairman, my boss, wanted us to get into juvenile programs, to the tune of $800,000," explains Director Tom Allison. "We have developed personnel efficiencies to such an extent that we can now go in and develop juvenile programming without asking for any additional money at all."

Privatization also continues to be a major change driver, particularly in Eastern Europe. As socialist or communist governments have been replaced by leaders with more free-market orientation, organizations have faced revolutionary changes demanded by privatization. Western Europe is not immune from this trend; in France alone, 1993 plans called for privatizing 21 companies to make them more competitive.[7]

4. *Internal need to improve performance and competitive situation.* While the external world creates many compelling needs for change, the internal one is the everyday reality for most organizations. Shareholder dissatisfaction, falling profits or market share, and threats to corporate survival itself command the most immediate attention. In Italy, for example, Pirelli Tire Company was facing bankruptcy in the 1990s because acquisitions in the 1980s had increased its debt to 1.5 times its equity. This "edge of destruction" scenario prompted changes that would otherwise have been unimaginable in the European climate, such as closing 12 plants, selling off a large division, leaving a swank corporate headquarters for a spare one, and downsizing 170 senior managers.[8]

The factors compelling change today have one more thing in common: They aren't going away. In fact, the majority of U.S. executives polled in the survey discussed above think the pace of change will accelerate from today's "rapid or extremely rapid" speed.[9]

7. Hofheinz, op. cit.
8. Hofheinz, op. cit.
9. Hammonds, op. cit.

CHANGE EFFORTS: SOME SUCCEED, MOST DO NOT

A variety of research suggests that, while some organizational change initiatives have produced desired process or outcome results, most conducted to date have failed to meet expectations. Some examples include:

- A Harvard University in-depth study of six large companies' experiences found that only one had made substantial changes toward revitalizing the company; three had made some of the desired changes; and two had actually decreased performance in change measures.[10]

- Of 133 companies trying to institute total quality management, only 29 percent said their satisfaction with their progress was high or very high; 50 percent had a moderate level of satisfaction; and 21 percent reported low or very low satisfaction. About half the most mature TQM programs (five-to-seven years old—only 22 companies of 133) said they were three-quarters of the way toward meeting the criteria for a Malcolm Baldrige Award.[11]

- Of 166 U.S. and European companies that are introducing changes, only about one-third reported success in most types of changes. For instance, 32 percent have been successful in changing vision/values/culture; 27 percent have succeeded in changing business systems/processes; and only 20 percent have successfully changed information technology.[12]

10. M. Beer et al., "Why Change Programs Don't Produce Change," *Harvard Business Review* (November/December 1990), pp. 158–166.

11. The Conference Board, *Employee Buy-In to Total Quality: A Corporate Progress Report* (New York: The Conference Board, 1991).

12. The Conference Board, *Change Management: An Overview of Current Initiatives* (New York: The Conference Board, 1994).

SUCCESSFUL CHANGE IS MANAGED CHANGE

What differentiates the change initiatives that succeed from those that fail? In each of the studies listed above, the organizations that were successful in making change also employed many of the effective strategies and techniques to manage change that the rest of this book will describe. In the Harvard study, for example, successful company revitalization was associated with improvements in interfunctional coordination, decision making, work organization, and concern for people. In the TQM study, respondents who scored themselves at or above the halfway mark for Baldrige award criteria placed more emphasis on communication, teams, employee feedback, and formal training programs. Participants in the study of companies introducing change said the most successful implementation tactics were maintaining a focus on change; ensuring consistent, intensive communication; developing process ownership; and tying change management to results. Those who were unsuccessful cited the need for better leadership training; the problem of uneven deployment of changes throughout a corporation; the inability to move initiatives from the senior executive level through lower-level managers; and internal politics and competition.

Analysis of Coopers & Lybrand's Organizational Assessment Program database of 400 international companies shows that 95 percent of those who had a data-driven change management program achieved the desired change and had positive results. Those who broke through the greatest number of barriers to change identified through organizational assessments realized the greatest improvements in business results.

A large electronics manufacturer in Austria is a good example of using change management techniques to make change—and better business results—happen. The company, which was implementing various changes to increase employee empowerment and customer orientation and improve profitability, had low organizational assessment scores on teamwork, motivation, and understanding goals. (The Coopers

& Lybrand database shows that scoring poorly in these areas is also negatively related to job satisfaction, morale, customer orientation, and quality.)

The company made plans to face each identified barrier to change. For example, the top 15 managers had in-depth meetings to consider the implications of poor company understanding of goals. They also identified the precise behavior needed to correct this problem: increased communication (which also could help promote teamwork and motivation). These managers then personally took the messages of goals and change to every plant in the company. The CEO set the tone for a new management style and increased worker involvement by taking the lead in communication. He told a large meeting of all headquarters employees, "Tomorrow we will be a different company. Your supervisors will respond differently to you and we expect you to act differently as well." He then outlined the nature of the desired changes and closed by saying, "If this is not true tomorrow, I want you to call me personally."

The day after this challenge he received hundreds of calls, which he followed up with managers and supervisors not yet on board with the change. By the end of the first week, the calls had begun to dwindle. He continued the pressure by having breakfast and lunch meetings with groups of employees, always asking whether management behaviors were changing and demonstrating how important employee input was under the new philosophy.

Following this communication strategy and other interventions, the company resurveyed the work force two years into the change process. The second survey showed substantial progress in overcoming initially identified barriers to change and in making desired changes such as an increase in customer orientation. At the same time, the company had increased its business by 200 percent and also increased its market share.

We could cite dozens more examples, but the principle remains the same: Experience shows that change does not happen on its own, and announcing a new order doesn't make it appear. Organizations that make real changes pay attention to managing the human, systems, and strategic factors that affect people's willingness and ability to change.

CHANGE MANAGEMENT: ORGANIZATIONS FACE SIMILAR CHALLENGES

The study cited earlier of companies introducing change shows that organizations face similar challenges in managing change. Change management initiatives receiving the highest "difficulty" scores included making changes in vision/values/culture (listed by 43 percent of companies); changing the decision-making process (35 percent); and changing leadership style (31 percent). Although 60 percent of study respondents tried to change leadership styles, only one-third claimed success. In his study of "Leadership, Empowerment, and Management Change," Warren Bennis reports that only 10 percent of corporations that change management styles institutionalize the new leadership; the rest revert to the old ways.[13]

Another research study confirms managers' particular difficulty in dealing with the human aspects of change. This study, which tested 700 executives on change management knowledge and skills, found that managers scored highest (although they still got a C, scoring between 70 and 79 percent) on measures like evaluating change, managing the organization side of change, and planning change. The scores fell to D levels (60 to 69 percent) for managing the people side of change, understanding the general nature of change, and their individual responses to change.[14] (See Exhibit 2.2.)

13. Warren Bennis, "Leadership, Empowerment, and Management Change" (internal Coopers & Lybrand point paper).

14. W. Warner Burke, "Managers Get a 'C' in Managing Change," *Training and Development Journal* (May 1991), pp. 87–92.

Exhibit 2.2

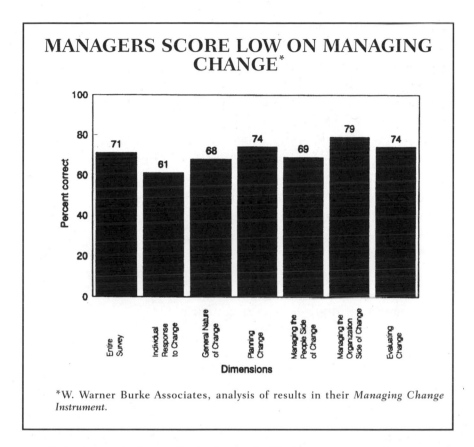

MANAGERS SCORE LOW ON MANAGING CHANGE*

*W. Warner Burke Associates, analysis of results in their *Managing Change Instrument.*

Other tests show that about half the executives are managers, rather than leaders. Yet leaders are the ones who have the qualities and capacities needed to manage change. (See Chap. 6 for further discussion.)

These trends strongly suggest that managers need better knowledge and skills to help organizations and people make the transition to new ways of doing business.

CHANGE MANAGERS: SLOWLY BUILDING TOWARD RESILIENCE

If change has become a constant, are organizations developing a constant capacity to manage it? Are they building in resilience? The evidence is conflicting, but the answer seems to be that many are trying to. For example, the ability of leaders to manage change is a critical aspect of an organization's capacity to deal with flux and adapt continuously, and the information reported above suggests that most executives do not yet have this ability. Yet, more than half of 166 U.S. and European companies introducing change say their firms are successfully building a capacity to manage change; only 10 percent say they have not been successful, and about one-third are uncertain how successful they've been.[15]

This study also found that most change efforts are relatively new: 60 percent began their initiatives in 1989 or later. Yet, successfully developing a single change can take three years or more, and developing fundamental organizational change management capabilities takes even longer. It is unrealistic to expect organizations struggling with initial changes to develop long-term capabilities right away. Fortunately, however, every change management activity organizations undertake can help them move toward permanent resilience.

CHANGE MANAGEMENT: NECESSARY, DIFFICULT, POSSIBLE

This brief review suggests that managing change is essential to making change happen regardless of national boundaries, and that many organizations are beginning to take the kinds of actions the rest of this book recommends and describes to help change succeed. Although organizations and managers are often uncomfortable in dealing with the human factors in change, they have begun to recognize how critical they are to success.

It is also clear that, even if change management is difficult, some organizations are proving that it can be done. Effective methods exist to manage change and, when properly

15. The Conference Board (1994), op. cit.

applied, they work. As the methodology we outline in Part 2 shows, change management is neither smoke and mirrors nor a theoretical exercise. It is a practical, data-driven process with concrete action steps and tools that produce measurable results.

MANAGING COMPLEX MAJOR CHANGES

This whole thing is really psychology. It's not really a technical problem. The higher you go in the company, the more people you find who have become successful by doing what they have always done. They have difficulty realizing the need to change their own habits. Another common problem is lack of a shared vision. If everyone is thinking about change in a slightly different way, it's very difficult to move the organization forward. You have to get the mental arrows lined up. Finally, there's lethargy. If you wait too long to do something, you may never do anything. But when people see change begin to happen—if some little thing is run up the flagpole and well received—then minds begin to change.

MIKE ROTHER, CONSULTANT

According to management consultants, only 5 percent of managers saw change as continuous and overlapping even 20 years ago. Today, 75 percent express that view. Caught in the vortex of fierce global competition and the ever-increasing speed of new technology, organizations find themselves in a situation where they can survive only by adapting, and adapting fast. Management guru Tom Peters does not even see the needed mutation as change anymore. "Eradicate 'change' from your vocabulary," he says. "Substitute 'revolution.'"[1] But change, or revolution, does not manage itself.[2] It needs to be planned, monitored, and nurtured.

1. Tom Peters, *The Tom Peters Seminar* (New York: Vintage Books, 1994), p. 3.

2. W. Warner Burke, *Organization Development: A Normative View* (Reading: Addison-Wesley, 1987), p. 121.

The Assess, Plan, Implement, Renew framework that Coopers & Lybrand's Change Management Services uses applies specific, proprietary tools and techniques to diagnose an organization's existing condition, develop a change process consistent with an organization's strategic goals, and involve and empower an organization's people toward a shared vision. (See Chap. 7 for detailed discussion.)

After years of experience with scores of clients, Coopers & Lybrand has found that this approach helps organizations perform activities that can make change happen. This chapter examines some of the most effective change levers:

- Organizing the change teams
- Reengineering a major process
- Managing a major market or technical transition
- Introducing a new management approach that requires major cultural change
- Building resilience

ORGANIZING THE CHANGE TEAMS

"We must all hang together, or assuredly we shall all hang separately," said Benjamin Franklin, a delegate to the Second Continental Congress. In fact, Franklin was a member of what may have been one of the first change teams. And it takes the kind of compelling need Franklin was talking about to galvanize a team and foster commitment.

Consultant Craig Schneier, interviewed for this book, observes, "When teams work, it doesn't matter if team members give 10 percent or 150 percent of their time, as long as they are committed to give their hearts and souls to the team." Remember the story about the pig and the chicken? They were debating the relative merits of bacon and eggs. "You know what the difference is between you and me?" asked the pig. "You're just interested, but I'm committed."

Teams can be a powerful accelerator to speed organizations to the nirvana of the high-involvement workplace. General Electric CEO Jack Welch, who has been credited with leading one of the biggest planned change efforts since China's Cultural Revolution,[3] told *Newsweek:*

> We believe right to our toes that we've got to engage every mind in this place. They've got to feel good about being here. They've got to feel their contributions are respected. That doesn't mean our standards aren't higher than ever in terms of productivity; we just happen to think this is the right way to do it. Breaking down boundaries, taking away hierarchy. The idea is to liberate people.[4]

A consultant who has worked with General Electric compares its team-based organization to the game of basketball, in which "you have to rely on real-time improvisation." The old organization, he says, was like the National Football League, with authoritarian coaches sending in plays to their teams and tightly defining everyone's role.[5]

AVOIDING THE ROLLING EYEBALL SYNDROME

Too often, people assigned to teams have the same complaint: "Everybody is talking big like they really want to get something done, but my boss rolls his eyes every time I have to go to one of these team meetings."

How can we boost the odds that teams will be able to drive change throughout the organization? Teams need the right sponsorship, the right mission, the right people, and the right performance measurement system.

---

3. Thomas A. Stewart, "GE Keeps Those Ideas Coming," *Fortune* (August 12, 1991), p. 41.

4. Jolie Solomon, "He Brought GE to Life," *Newsweek* (November 30, 1992), p. 63.

5. Joseph Weber, "Letting Go Is Hard to Do," *BusinessWeek* (special enterprise issue, October 22, 1993), p. 219.

In other words, the mandate for teams has to come from the top of the organization. The task has to be complex, with multiple possible paths to the objective, cross-hierarchical or functional boundaries, and a rich database. Team members have to be recognized leaders recruited from among the best and brightest staff and line people, and they have to be trained in how to collaborate, listen, set agendas, obtain information, solve problems, and make decisions.

Teams have to be charged with setting targets that are outrageous but achievable, based on benchmarking. Examples might include doubling revenue while cutting costs in half, cutting cycle time in half, or cutting new product development time by three-quarters. Stretch targets will pull team members out of their comfort zones—their boxes on the organization chart—and demand new ways of thinking.[6]

TEAM DYNAMICS

Organizational development specialists segment a team's life cycle into four phases:

- Phase I: Team members get to know and assess each other.
- Phase II: First clashes occur on how to accomplish goals.
- Phase III: Team members begin to agree on strategy and means.
- Phase IV: The team becomes productive.

In *The Professional Manager,* Douglas McGregor gives a detailed analysis of how teams work.[7] After research, observations, and many consulting assignments, he identified what he considers key success factors:

---

6. David P. Allen, assistant vice president of benchmarking initiatives, GTE Telephone Operations, interview.

7. Douglas McGregor, *The Professional Manager* (New York: McGraw-Hill, 1967).

- *Clear understanding and mutual agreement.* The team's primary task and how to accomplish it must be fully understood and accepted by every team member.

- *Open communications.* Physicist David Bohm differentiates between the two primary types of discourse. Discussion has the same root as percussion and concussion and suggests a Ping-Pong game where winning is the objective. Dialogue, on the other hand, comes from the Greek *dialogos*. *Dia* means through, and *logos* means the word. Through the word, expressed as divergent individual views, team members can look out through each other's unique individual perspectives, and the team as a group can gain insights that cannot be accessed individually. This is an opening-up type of consensus. A focusing-down consensus seeks the team's common denominator and rejects views that all do not share; it is a powerful force that tends to make the intelligence of the team less than the intelligence of individual team members.

  It is also essential that the physical setting be conducive to open communications among members of the team. Exhibit 3.1 provides an example of this principle in action.

- *Mutual trust.* As Douglas McGregor writes, this fundamental premise can be summarized as follows: "I know that you will not—deliberately or accidentally, consciously or unconsciously—take unfair advantage of me. I can put my situation at the moment, my status and self-esteem in this group, our relationship, my job, my career, even my life, in your hands with complete confidence."

- *Mutual support.* This essential adjunct to mutual trust is characterized by the absence of hostility and indifference and the presence of concern and active help toward one another.

- *Management of human differences.* Great teams have conflict, maintains Peter Senge in *The Fifth Discipline*. Senge, who is director of the Systems Thinking and Organizational Learning Program at MIT's Sloan School of Management and a consultant to major corporations, points out that

Exhibit 3.1

INSIDE THE TEAM ROOM

"All team members must live together," proclaims Tom Peters. Space management is the issue, and Peters contends even thin walls or a few dozen feet of open space will block communication.* The notion behind teams is breaking barriers. As the poet Robert Frost wrote, "Something there is that doesn't love a wall."

When a large investment firm moved its back-office support organization out of its New York City headquarters to a southeastern city, everything was redesigned: processes, technology, titles, evaluations, and furniture.

Explains the managing director, U.S. operations:

> We believe in teams, so the furniture had to have low barriers. A typical job family will have about 10 people facing each other, with a conversation pit with swivel chairs located in the middle.

> That facilitates high performance, because people who are doing similar jobs can see and talk to each other. In New York, we were all in cubicles surrounded by high barriers. If you wanted to talk to somebody, you had to stand up or just shout.**

*Tom Peters, *Thriving on Chaos: Handbook for a Management Revolution* (New York: Knopf, 1987), p. 263.
**Marc Sternfeld, managing director, U.S. operations, Salomon Brothers Inc., interview.

---

mediocre teams usually display no signs of conflict because team members are suppressing their views or because there is rigid polarization—everyone knows where everyone else stands and there is little movement. The trick is to use dialogue to transform potentially destructive conflict into productive energy that will propel the emergence of a shared vision from different personal visions.[8]

- *Selective use of the team.* Teams need high maintenance. If there is a single, clean, albeit complex, task to perform, individuals may be the best answer. As is often noted, "Democracy is painfully inefficient, but it can be quite effective."[9] Don't forget, it took the Second Continental Congress a year to come up with the Declaration of Independence.

- *Appropriate member skills.* These must include technical knowledge to accomplish the task, and, just as necessary, team-building proficiency. As Senge explains, one of the most useful team-building skills is "the ability to recognize when people are *not* reflecting on their own assumptions, when they are *not* inquiring into each other's thinking, when they are *not* exposing their thinking in a way that encourages others to inquire into it."[10]

  Embracing internal and external suppliers and customers on the team is also important. Team Taurus was the Ford Motor Company's new product development group responsible for creating a car that not only won awards for design and quality but came in under the product development budget by almost $500 million.

  Ford people from design and engineering, production, purchasing, sales and marketing, and legal and dealer service departments worked side by side, along with suppliers. Breaking with tradition, some suppliers submitted designs for the component parts they had become so expert in manufacturing. Dealers and potential new car buyers were also involved in the product development process.[11]

- *Leadership.* Teams should move toward self-management.

---

8. Peter Senge, *The Fifth Discipline: The Art and Practice of the Learning Organization* (New York: Doubleday, 1990).

9. Craig Schneier, Craig Eric Schneier Associates, interview.

10. Senge, op. cit., p. 256.

11. Tom Peters, *Thriving on Chaos: Handbook for a Management Revolution* (New York: Knopf, 1987).

t in the early stages of the team life cycle, a masterful
ilitator will help ensure that key success factors are in
place, while guarding against becoming the "answer man,"
whose ideas and responsibilities supersede those of other
team members.[12]

- *Accountability.* Finally, accountability in the form of pay-for-
performance or some other reward system has to be built
into the team. There is a major difference between being
supportive of change and being held accountable for its success. Unless the destiny of each team member depends on
the performance of all team members, there will not be a
team. It may be a communications network or a reporting
vehicle or a coffee klatch masquerading as a team, but it
will not be a team.

Even when all these steps have been taken and safeguards
established, there is no guarantee that a team will function
well. A team in which individuals are engaged in glossing over
problems and not in checking for root problems will not be
effective. Another trap that change-management-conscious
executives easily walk into is thinking that teams can be the
answer to every step of every process in an organization. There
are still responsibilities and tasks—such as some R&D—that
are best assumed by individuals.

REENGINEERING A MAJOR PROCESS

Work processes link high-performance teams and the organization at large by cutting through the barriers separating the
traditional silos of the vertical organization: design, engineering, manufacturing, purchasing, marketing, and sales. At the
same time, work processes directly link the team and the organization to the customer by flowing outside the organization
and delivering the organization's goods and services.

Lawrence Bossidy, CEO of AlliedSignal, says, "There is a

---

12. Senge, op. cit., pp. 246–247.

nearly unanimous opinion forming that in the 1990s we'll be running businesses primarily by customer-oriented processes."[13] Watching and working with customers at their place of employment, say Michael Hammer and James Champy in *Reengineering the Corporation,* are the best ways to answer questions about customer requirements and problems. Interviews in conference rooms generally will elicit responses that do not reflect what customers actually do or will tend to focus on predictable and nonspecific requests for improvements in delivery time, quality, and pricing.

Understanding how an organization's goods and services help or hinder its success begins to shed light on how work processes should be designed and implemented to add value— from the customer's perspective—to those goods and services. A significant part of process reengineering, then, lies not so much in analyzing existing processes but in understanding how work should be done and why. Companies successful at improving processes are the ones that learn how to do their work better.

The Change Map

Coopers & Lybrand management consultants find three initiatives critical in managing process reengineering:

1. Building people's commitment to change
2. Designing the organization to make the process changes work
3. Enabling continuous improvement to sustain the change

Only top management sees the big picture that reengineering demands, and only top management has the necessary authority over multiple departments to drive process change through the organization. Line employees and middle man-

---

13. Stratford Sherman, "A Master Class in Radical Change," *Fortune* (December 13, 1993), p. 84.

agers may know more than anyone about problems in their own segment, but they are not in the best position to see the entire process. They may also justifiably resist any change because the reengineered process can result in a loss of their power, influence, authority, or even jobs.[14]

This is why Coopers & Lybrand centers its reengineering efforts on the organization's leaders. The first step is to identify the drivers of successful reengineering and what actions will overcome resistance and win commitment to change. The resulting strategy and action plan, called the Change Map (see Exhibit 3.2), addresses these issues:

- Integrating elements of organizational strategy as the framework for change
- Setting ambitious performance objectives for the change and actively monitoring progress
- Providing substantial resources to the change effort
- Removing barriers to change
- Communicating a compelling need for change to build commitment at all organizational levels
- Building an infrastructure for change

THE POWER OF ONE

When the fourth largest publicly owned telecommunications company in the world embarked on one of the most massive process reengineering projects ever undertaken,[15] internal communications played a leading role.

Says an assistant vice president, "We had to create linkage between the hard deliverables—technology and process—and the softer needs of people to understand where they fit in,

14. James Champy and Michael Hammer, *Reengineering the Corporation* (New York: Harper Business, 1993), pp. 207–212.

15. David P. Allen and Robert Nafius, "Dreaming and Doing: Reengineering GTE Telephone Operations," *Planning Review* (March/April 1993), pp. 28–29.

Exhibit 3.2

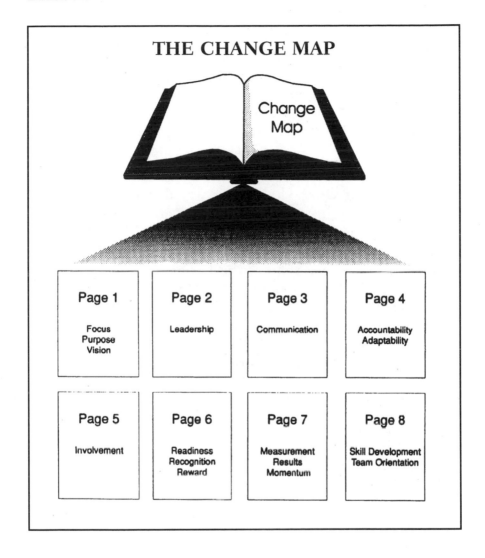

where the new process fits in, how it works organizationally, and how it's going to look. Perhaps most important was how to enroll people to gain buy-in and participation."

The Power of One, a communications program, reinforced the message of one team, one vision, one attitude. Deregulation had subjected 30 percent of the company's businesses to competitive pressure. Projections forecasted deregulation would spread to 70 percent of the company during the next six years. People had to accept the need to cut costs, to change or die, to build customer-in to customer-out processes—without feeling that the company was out only to axe jobs and fatten its bottom line.

DIAL 1-800-Q&A-BOSS

How does an organization get almost 100,000 employees in widely dispersed locations in more than 60 divisions to believe in the Power of One? The answer was downlink broad-band television. Using this technology, senior officers communicated companywide in real time.

An officer of the company reports, "We rapidly learned the more information we shared, the better off we were in persuading people that we should, could, and would take reengineering forward." At the end of these live, extemporaneous sessions, viewers can call an 800 number or a fax line and communicate directly with the bosses.

Employee surveys are another way to take the organizational pulse. They ask questions like, "Have you heard of reengineering?" "Do you know what it is?" "Do you support it?" "Do you think it's necessary for the company to change radically?" Responses during the first three years of reengineering show decreasing resistance as more and more people participate in change.

Example: customer care centers. The idea behind this innovation is to give the first person who talks to the customer the information, tools, and technology necessary to satisfy a customer's repair need 70 percent of the time on the first call. After six months, two pilot sites in live customer contact locations were able to satisfy customer complaints 35 to 40 percent of the time on the first call. The company standard *had* been 0.5 percent.

For the customer contact team that reengineered this customer service process, and for other teams that have reengineered other organizational processes, seeing is believing. An assistant vice president proudly states, "People were anxious they could never achieve breakthroughs because they were just telephone people, but given the right tools and put in the right environment, they were able to reach down inside themselves and come up with truly revolutionary approaches to our business."[16]

MANAGING A MAJOR MARKET OR TECHNICAL TRANSITION

Too often, organizations invest millions—or billions—of dollars in information technology and get only marginal productivity improvements. Information technology enables organizations to reengineer processes and make other radical changes in how work is done. (See Exhibit 3.3.)

Yet careful planning has to take place and consideration must be given to how the new system will affect the people and the organization.

The debut of the London Ambulance Service's computer-aided dispatch system was greeted by press accounts of unnecessary deaths because ambulances arrived late or not at all. Once again, technology had failed—with a high price. Or had it? Closer inspection revealed that management had virtually dumped the new system on its people. They were expected to align themselves with the technology almost spontaneously with no management intervention.

The unplanned implications were significant. People were working in unfamiliar positions, segregated from colleagues with whom they had jointly solved problems before, and without paper backup. In short, the new system eliminated one of the powerful facilitators of change management—teams.[17]

TECHNOLOGY CHANGE = CULTURE CHANGE

Technology, which underpins organizational culture, has become a load-bearing structure. Replace it at your own risk.

---

16. Allen interview.

17. Michael Kenward, "Technology with a Human Face," *Director* (October 1993), p. 27.

Exhibit 3.3

TECHNOLOGICAL SIDE EFFECTS: EMPOWERING SUPPLIERS AND CUSTOMERS

What happens when you throw a rock into a pond? Ripples of energy spread outward over the body of water. Introducing a new technology into an organization also makes waves that can push through the organization and reach suppliers and customers. Although not necessarily the primary reason that technology was introduced in the first place, these side effects are sometimes more interesting. Two examples:

- Vendors supplying parts to General Motors's Saturn plant can access the plant's manufacturing database, consult the production schedule, and deliver the appropriate parts—with no purchase order or invoice—in boxes printed with bar codes that initiate payment when the receiving clerk scans them with an electric wand. Result? Vendors can plan their production and shipping schedule weeks in advance.[*]

- Boston Chicken's customers will soon be able to use a touch-activated computer terminal to rate the quality of food and service. Result? Says the head of computer operations, "If I can know almost instantaneously that customers don't like the drink selection and I can have that changed in 300 stores within a week—that's worth a whole lot of money."[**]

[*]Champy and Hammer, op. cit.

[**]Steven Pearlstein, "Boston Chicken: Hot Stuff," *The Washington Post* (July 4, 1994), p. A9.

The best companies get ready for change early and anticipate the implications of new technology.

When Wayne Gretzky was asked what made him a great hockey player, he replied, "I go where the puck is going to be, not where it is." The same principle governs formulating a technology strategy.[18] The question is not, "How can existing technology improve existing processes?"[19] but rather, "What would a process look like if there were a technology that allowed us to break away from the old ways of doing work?" In other words, process drives the technology strategy—not the other way around.[20]

As Hammer and Champy point out, "It takes time to study [technology], to understand its significance, to conceptualize its potential uses, to sell those uses inside the company, and to plan the deployment. An organization that can execute these preliminaries before the technology actually becomes available will inevitably gain a significant lead on its competition—in many cases, three years or more."[21]

Technological Transformation

The Xerox Corporation is in the middle of a technological transformation that is revolutionizing its business, according to Chairman and CEO Paul Allaire. Says Allaire, "It is changing the skills our employees need, the competitors we face—and, indeed, the very nature of the business we are in."

Xerox's traditional business is copiers and duplicators. But with the emergence of competitively priced digital technology, the electro-optical mechanisms in copiers are being replaced with scanning devices that digitize the information on the page and capture the image electronically.

Now the company that dominated world copier markets in

---

18. Champy and Hammer, op. cit., p. 100.

19. Champy and Hammer, op. cit., p. 85.

20. Allen interview.

21. Champy and Hammer, op. cit., pp. 100–101.

the 1960s and lost half its market share to low-cost Japanese competitors 20 years later is in the business of managing electronic and paper documents—manipulating document color, enhancing document quality, embedding photographs in documents, merging electronic documents transmitted over a network with paper documents, storing documents electronically, and sending documents electronically to be printed at a remote location.

Increasingly, says Allaire, Xerox is entering markets dominated by computer systems businesses or printing companies. The strategy:

- *Redefine hardware*—the business planning system, control mechanisms, measurements systems, reporting relationships, and other processes.

- *Redefine people skills*—the 23 characteristics needed by the ideal manager at the new Xerox.

- *Redefine software*—the value system, culture, and other informal networks and practices that link people. Cautions Allaire, "This is probably the most important component. Any company that leaves this out of its organizational change effort is making a big mistake."[22]

INTRODUCING A NEW MANAGEMENT APPROACH THAT REQUIRES MAJOR CULTURE CHANGE

The proliferation of teams, the shift in emphasis from vertical structures to horizontal processes, advances in technology— all these changes demand new approaches to managing. The best organizations realize that change is continuous and overlapping. They spend more time managing innovation than becoming better at what they are already doing.

---

22. Robert Howard, "The CEO as Organizational Architect: An Interview with Xerox's Paul Allaire," *Harvard Business Review* (September/October 1992), pp. 107–121.

Declares General Electric's Welch, "My job is to listen to, search for, think of, and spread ideas, to expose people to good ideas and role models."[23]

At the global technology organization in General Electric's lighting business, a multidisciplinary senior leadership group of about 10 people allocates resources and ensures coordination of nearly 100 worldwide processes or programs. "They stay away from the day-to-day activities, which are managed by the teams themselves," says the human resources manager.[24]

Instead of bosses designing and allocating work, members do that for themselves; they also don't need to be supervised and controlled as they establish their own built-in control system. So what does the new boss do? Here are some examples:

- Influence and reinforce employee values and beliefs
- Ensure that performance measurement and compensation systems reward results that reflect desired values and beliefs
- Develop hiring criteria that evaluate character, self-discipline, motivation, and initiative as well as education, training, and skills
- Build organizational capacity through education that promotes employees' insight and understanding of the "why," rather than only giving them training that stresses the "how"[25]

LIGHTS, CAMERA, ACTION!

As is often observed, we live in a visual age, and more and more organizations are using visual aids to introduce new ideas and role models, facilitate change in management

---

23. Stratford Sherman, "A Master Class in Radical Change," *Fortune* (December 13, 1993), p. 83.

24. John A. Byrne, "The Horizontal Corporation: It's about Managing Across, Not Up and Down," *BusinessWeek* (December 20, 1993), pp. 76–81.

25. Champy and Hammer, op. cit., pp. 71–79.

approaches, and align employee behavior with desired values and beliefs.

In Southern California, a boat-building company with a predominantly unskilled immigrant work force conquered a problem with production efficiency. At first, management performed a variation of the old time-and-motion study, using a stopwatch to analyze productivity. "It went over like a concrete cloud," declares the company president. Then he persuaded teams to videotape themselves. Like sports teams, employees had a designated film room where they studied the videotapes and brainstormed improvements.

"The key to success," says the president of the company, "was respecting the suggestions workers made. If I'd been the one to tell them they were wasting a lot of time, I'd have gotten less than a positive response." Some suggestions were implemented; others were not. But videotaping has become an iterative process to build continuous improvement. Results: After one year of videotaping and instituting other changes, the time to complete one boat fell from 25 days to five, and direct labor decreased by 800 man-hours.[26]

BUILDING RESILIENCE

Continuous improvement is an integral element in what is known as the "learning organization"[27]—and in the way Coopers & Lybrand thinks about change management.

After the gain—and pain—of change, there is a natural inclination to take a breather. However, it is precisely when an organization begins to realize its objectives and establishes new standards that competitors begin to benchmark against these new standards. To face this situation and come out on the winning side, organizations have to integrate ongoing improvement. In other words, developing the capacity to remain *continuously* adaptable and resilient is the answer. (See Exhibit 3.4.)

26. Paul Lazarus, "Reorganizing the Manufacturing Plant," *Professional BoatBuilder* (June/July 1994), pp. 22–25; Paul Hebert interview.
27. Senge, op. cit.

Exhibit 3.4

CHARACTERISTICS OF AN ADAPTIVE CULTURE

W. Warner Burke, a consultant and professor of psychology and education at Columbia University, often works with Coopers & Lybrand on change management projects. He underscores the value of organizational flexibility—what he calls "adaptive culture." Here are the hallmarks of organizations that can reconfigure themselves to meet the changing interests of stockholders, customers, and employees:

- Willingness to make changes in culturally ingrained behaviors
- Emphasis on identifying problems before they occur and rapidly implementing workable solutions
- Focus on innovation
- Shared feeling of confidence regarding managing problems and opportunities
- Emphasis on trust
- Willingness to take risks
- Spirit of enthusiasm—doing whatever it takes to achieve organizational success
- Candidness
- Internal flexibility in response to external demands
- Consistency in word and action
- Long-term focus*

*W. Warner Burke, *The Burke-Litwin Model: Master Class*, participant manual, 1994.

Consultant and psychologist Daryl Conner, who collaborates with Coopers & Lybrand, says "The single most important factor in managing change successfully is the degree to which people demonstrate resilience: the ability to absorb high levels of disruptive change while displaying minimal dysfunctional behavior."[28] (See Exhibit 3.5.)

Resilience can be measured. It rests on a sturdy tripod of capability building, people empowerment, and culture change. Capability building and people empowerment involve establishing monitoring processes and reassessment techniques, team effectiveness, problem-solving skills, proficiency in cultural management, leadership expertise, and organizational communication.

28. Daryl R. Conner, *Managing at the Speed of Change* (New York: Villard Books, 1993), p. 60.

Exhibit 3.5

FIVE ATTRIBUTES OF RESILIENCE

In *Managing at the Speed of Change,* Daryl Conner details the five characteristics and associated beliefs, behaviors, skills, and knowledge required to raise the threshold for "future shock":

Positive—Views Life as Challenging but Opportunity-Filled

- Interprets the world as multifaceted and overlapping
- Expects the future to be filled with constantly shifting variables
- Views disruptions as the natural state of a changing world
- Sees life as filled with more paradoxes than contradictions
- Sees major change as uncomfortable, but believes that hidden opportunities may actually exist
- Believes there are usually important lessons to be learned from challenges
- Sees life as generally rewarding

Focused—Clear Vision of What Is to Be Achieved

- Maintains a strong vision that serves both as a source of purpose and as a guidance system to reestablish perspectives following significant disruption

Exhibit 3.5 (*Continued*)

Flexible—Pliable When Responding to Uncertainty

- Believes change is a manageable process
- Has a high tolerance for ambiguity
- Needs only a short time to recover from adversity or disappointment
- Feels empowered during change
- Recognizes strengths and weaknesses and knows when to accept internal or external limits
- Challenges and, when necessary, modifies, assumptions or frames of reference
- Relies on nurturing relationships for support
- Displays patience, understanding, and humor when dealing with change

Organized—Applies Structures to Help Manage Ambiguity

- Identifies the underlying themes embedded in confusing situations
- Consolidates what appear to be several unrelated change projects into a single effort with a central theme
- Sets and, when necessary, renegotiates, priorities during change
- Manages many simultaneous tasks and demands successfully
- Compartmentalizes stress in one area so that it does not carry over to other projects or parts of life
- Recognizes when to ask others for help
- Takes major action only after careful planning

Exhibit 3.5 (*Continued*)

Proactive—Engages Change Instead of Evading It

- Determines when a change is inevitable, necessary, or advantageous
- Uses resources to creatively reframe a changing situation, improvise new approaches, and maneuver to gain advantage
- Takes risks despite potentially negative consequences
- Draws important lessons from change-related experiences that are then applied to similar situations
- Responds to disruption by investing energy in problem solving and teamwork
- Influences others and resolves conflicts*

*Daryl R. Conner, *Managing at the Speed of Change* (New York: Villard Books, 1993), pp. 238–240.

UNDERSTANDING THE HUMAN CHANGE PROCESS

Although we did take some steps to prepare for change, we did not start with a formal plan to address the human aspects of change. It would have been a great idea. Hindsight tells us we should have done more to develop a plan first.

J. M. SHAFER, SOUTHWESTERN POWER ADMINISTRATION

PREPARING FOR CHANGE

No element is as crucial in an organization, as important to its good functioning, its success or failure, its survival or demise, as the human one. The new managers emerging in the business world know this. They give it priority in their projected changes in terms of anticipating how the changes are going to affect the work force and preparing for that. In fact, managing the work force during a change period is the essential component of change management.

In any individual, the need to change may arise for different reasons. A person may realize that a change in lifestyle is in order after a heart attack, for example. Or the need for a change in behavior may become apparent as a result of increasingly poor interpersonal relationships. Alternatively, the need may become clear as the result of an external event like the abrupt ending of a marriage or a change in management at work. A change in the workplace in these difficult economic times can cause stress and anxiety if not downright fear for job security.

Change is generally defined as a significant disruption in established patterns of behavior and/or expectations. The significance of the degree of change is measured mainly by how it is perceived by those affected by it—as well as by how they react to it. What is perceived as a major change by one person may appear insignificant to another. The components of human response to change are complex. However, some that can be readily distinguished are: unwillingness to chart new territories, a perceived or real threat to job security, accustomation to the current culture, and lethargy. Human beings are conservative by nature. Children, who refuse any change in their rituals, are the best example of this reality, until, in the process of growing up, they learn that nothing remains static. It is a fact of life that some rare individuals accept change readily and indeed seem to thrive on it, but the vast majority of people resist it until they realize what the animal kingdom has known for millions of years: Adapt or disappear.

This chapter will concentrate on accepting the inevitability of change, assessing its effect, and easing the process.

READINESS FOR CHANGE

In the workplace, since time immemorial, employees or workers have been suspicious of management and felt threatened by it, in the belief that decisions are never made in the best interests of those who do the work but of those who manage it. Until a generation ago, workers were told to obey, and a strict system of reward and punishment prevented them from doing otherwise. Managers, in turn—even relatively enlightened ones—tended to see all workers as ready to cheat on work hours, benefits, and quality of work whenever given the chance.

To both sides, the others were "them," always up to no good, and invisible barriers separated the two. In the present context, communication has started circulating differently, and managers as well as workers acknowledge a "you." In the best of cases, the work force of an organization is composed of "us."

In order for that point to be reached, however, information must be widely disseminated, and communication must flow easily. Organizational change always appears threatening to the work force, if only in terms of job security. People preparing for change ought to understand the need for it. It is difficult to suppress all negative feelings on the part of a work force that, after all, often foresees major downsizing as a result of the change effort. But if leaders take the trouble to share with employees the difficulties of the transitional period that all organizations go through, a much higher degree of commitment and involvement can be obtained. A leadership expecting people to change must explain the reasons for the change as well as the consequences of not changing.

SAYING GOOD-BYE TO THE PAST

It is human nature to glorify the past, and employees will tend to do it even if the way things used to be done is the reason the company has to make drastic changes. Management would be wise to deal with this human aspect before forcing employees to move into new and uncharted territory.

People also naturally want to complete unfinished business and will spend energy trying to deal with the incompleteness, which may take the form of criticizing new procedures or even sabotaging them. This is part of the defensive strategies of resistance to change which, as W. Warner Burke says, may "reflect energy devoted to closure attempts. Providing some way for organizational members to disengage, to finish the past...helps them to focus on the change and the future."[1]

REACTIONS TO CHANGE

People are affected by change to varying degrees, depending on a number of factors in their professional and personal lives. Both size and speed make a difference. Contrary to what one might believe, it is not necessarily true that the bigger the change, the more difficult it is for people to accept it. (See Exhibit 4.1.) Sometimes a major change is easier to bear than

1. W. Warner Burke, *Organization Development: A Normative View* (Reading, Mass.: Addison-Wesley, 1987), p. 118.

Exhibit 4.1

UNIFORMS AND PARKING SPACE AT COMALCO

Comalco is a rolled products company based in New South Wales, Australia, that does extensive change management training with Coopers & Lybrand. Here is how Justin O'Connell describes the work force's response to some of the changes the company made:

> We were experimenting with a form of communication; we were trying to change the way people looked at work. In fact, it was an interesting period, for the Training Guarantee Act handed down certain percentages of payroll to spend on training. For us, it was up to 15 percent at one stage. That's a lot of money. The bulk of that went to nontechnical training, to team skills, for example. We tried to develop a sense of where we wanted to go as an organization and then attack symbols that weren't congruent with that. For example, at that stage there were probably five types of uniforms on the site: for electricians, fitters, operators, foremen, etc. Another thing was that all the managers, or anyone with a company car, would be parked in one parking [lot], and everyone else in others. A third thing was that the work force had to clock on, but not staff people. We got rid of the clocking-on requirements, we got rid of the separate uniforms, and we got rid of the differential carpark.
>
> We did other things as well. We spent money on change houses; we went to people and asked, "What are the things that upset you in your work?" and then we spent time changing those things.

Exhibit 4.1 (*Continued*)

The outcome was different from what we expected. We had naively thought that when we took these steps, people would be pleased. Everything we did was strongly opposed. When we removed the clocking-on system, people said, "We won't be able to prove that we've been to work, so they'll be able to cheat us in our pay," or, "We'll be all right, but others will cheat the system." As for managers parking their cars with everyone else, people said that the reason was that the managers' cars would be less visible and people wouldn't see when they had a new car, and so on. So there were all these myths going around, all these rumors that this and that was going to happen, and when it didn't, our credibility as management started improving.*

*Justin O'Connell, Comalco, interview.

---

a small one because so little about the new endeavor is similar to the old one. Therefore, there is less baggage to carry along to possibly impede the progress of change.

The speed or suddenness of the change is also a factor. Often, the slower the change, the more it hurts. By the same token, the longer people have to ruminate on the future, the more time they have to build up anger, fear, and resentment. The sooner the change is accomplished and people begin to understand what is expected of them, practice their new roles, and actually reach some of them, the sooner they will be able to come to grips with the reality of the change and the effect it will have on their lives. And reality almost always dispels the type of free-floating anxiety that accompanies change.

Values, the core element of corporate culture, are difficult to change. In fact, it is often easier and more productive not to try to change values, but rather to emphasize the values that are consistent with the proposed changes and to de-emphasize those that are not. Such decisions must come from corporate leadership, which must communicate them to employees—not by fiat, but rather by providing ways for employees to accept the desired culture and by personally demonstrating corporate values.

According to Dan Stolle, director of human resources at Tellabs, "The part of change that people have the most difficulty with is when the change affects their personal situation. Sometimes it's as simple as having to move their office."[2]

Changing the composition of the work force—that is, requiring that employees work with different people, also provokes strong reactions. Employees accustomed to participating in one kind of environment will feel insecure when asked to make a shift in their habitual work relationships.

An individual's gain or loss of power within an organization also has a tremendous effect on the change management process. When essential structures and functions are altered, it is inevitable that some people, especially those in middle management, will lose power. Once again, good communication will help alleviate some of the anger and resentment.

RESISTANCE TO CHANGE

Peter Senge says that whenever there is resistance to change, there are also hidden balancing processes. Resistance, says Senge, "is neither capricious nor mysterious. It almost always arises from threats to traditional norms and ways of doing things. Often these norms are woven into the fabric of established power relationships. The norm is entrenched because the distribution of authority and control is entrenched. Rather than pushing harder to overcome resistance to change, artful leaders discern the source of the resistance. They focus direct-

2. Dan Stolle, director of human resources, Tellabs, interview.

ly on the implicit norms and power relationships within which the norms are embedded."[3]

Managers find that resistance may be the major problem accompanying organizational change. John Gamba, senior vice president, corporate and human resources, Bell Atlantic, says, "People operate at certain comfort levels. This leads to inertia sometimes, as well as a fear of anything new. Getting people to change the way they regard their work or the way they solve problems is the most difficult part of the change management process."[4]

Management experts find the fault often lies with the idea that every member of an organization must adopt an upbeat attitude no matter what the circumstances. Chris Argyris, a Harvard professor who closely monitors workplace issues, finds that the emphasis on positive thinking is counterproductive. "It overlooks the critical role that dissatisfaction, low morale, and negative attitudes can play—often *should* play—in giving an accurate picture of organizational reality, especially with regard to threatening or sensitive issues. (For example, if employees are helping to eliminate their own jobs, why should we expect or encourage them to display high morale or disguise their mixed feelings?)"[5] This attitude also condescendingly assumes that employees can only function in a cheerful atmosphere, whereas executives are allowed mood swings and negative responses to problems.

Resistance to change is mainly an effort to maintain the status quo. According to Daryl Conner, it is also true that "the fear and ambiguity and loss of control during change is so powerful that it immobilizes many people and prevents their movement to even highly desired new circumstances."[6]

---

3. Peter M. Senge, *The Fifth Discipline: The Art and Practice of the Learning Organization* (New York: Doubleday, 1990), p. 88.

4. John Gamba, senior vice president, corporate and human resources, Bell Atlantic, interview.

5. Chris Argyris, "Good Communication That Blocks Learning," *Harvard Business Review* (July/August 1994), p. 77–85.

6. Daryl R. Conner, *Managing at the Speed of Change* (New York: Villard Books, 1993).

Human beings spend their lives resisting change. That they should resist it when perceiving a present or future difference in their work environment is not necessarily a negative phenomenon. For an organization to fail to recognize and deal constructively with resistance will have more far-reaching consequences.

Resistance can manifest itself in a number of ways, from generally negative attitudes to outright sabotage of the company's products and/or services. The two best ways to avoid these destructive consequences are to assess potential resistance at the outset of the planned change (by conducting individual or group interviews and surveys to measure employee resistance or readiness), and to prevent seriously harmful resistance by involving all employees in the change management process. Coopers & Lybrand consultants use tools and techniques further described in Chap. 7 that can be part of effective strategies to prevent and overcome resistance. These strategies include:

- Communicating often with management and employees and fully and honestly describing the changes that will take place as well as the reasons for them
- Assessing employee readiness for change
- Removing unnecessary barriers to change, such as rules and regulations that make no sense in view of the planned changes
- Engaging in test projects to determine the effectiveness of change—and then reporting the results of those projects to all employees (even if the results are not the ones anticipated)
- Demonstrating leadership's commitment to change by engaging in behaviors desired of employees, and making it clear that management is totally committed to the change and expects the employees to be as well
- Developing ways to help make the proposed changes more acceptable (even desirable) to employees

- Maintaining absolute honesty and integrity at all times
- Determining in advance exactly how employees will have to change and what they will have to do to ensure success for the planned changes
- Involving employees in the planned changes as much as possible—that is, encouraging them to adopt a positive attitude by giving them a vested interest in success
- Developing human resource policies that support the planned changes
- Providing ongoing training and education to ensure that employees have the skills necessary to make the changes
- Rewarding desired behavior and establishing disincentives for undesired behavior

In their book *Changing the Essence,* Richard Beckhard and Wendy Pritchard suggest developing a commitment plan and implementing strategies that will achieve desired results. Some of the options include:

- Establishing a mechanism to identify problems
- Instituting educational activities for managing organizational change and helping people understand the reasons for the changes
- Ensuring that the organizational leadership demonstrate its own commitment to change
- Changing the reward system by rewarding desired behaviors
- Encouraging collaboration even when people have widely different ideas and knowledge bases
- Improving communication strategies[7]

---

7. Richard Beckhard and Wendy Pritchard, *Changing the Essence: The Art of Creating and Leading Fundamental Change in Organizations* (San Francisco: Jossey-Bass, 1992), pp. 79–84.

BUILDING RESILIENCE

Most people take technological and scientific changes in stride, probably because their effect on their day-to-day lives is gradual and marginal. However, a 50-year-old executive who thinks about what it was like to make a long-distance phone call when he or she was a child and compares it to the current ability to create a document in English in New York, have a computer encode it, press a button, and watch it come out in Tokyo on paper—in Japanese—could be forgiven for feeling a little overwhelmed. Developing resilience in the face of the many changes we face is essential.

When discussing the major changes his company was making, one executive made the following observation about the turmoil: "My dad used to say that if you swing long enough, you get used to hanging!"

Fortunately, organizations do not require their employees to demonstrate that kind of resilience, although organizational changes may sometimes feel a little like a death sentence, at least until they're understood.

EMPOWERMENT

An effective way for a company to help its employees develop resilience is to empower them in their work. "Empowerment" has turned into a buzzword of the 1990s and, as such, its meaning has become oversimplified and incorrectly used in business. According to T. Wood Parker, a Coopers & Lybrand consultant, "Empowerment is one of the least understood words in modern management, guaranteed to raise the hackles of many managers and reasonable expectations among employees. A popular (and simplistic) notion is that it means 'managers authorize workers to make decisions.'"[8]

Parker says this is not necessarily the case. He sees empowerment as an enabling factor—that is, employees are given the skills and tools to be able to control many aspects of

---

8. T. Wood Parker, consultant, Coopers & Lybrand.

their own jobs. For example, "Employers are setting up self-managed teams of employees to control daily operations in their work processes; besides doing the work, they also prepare production schedules, order supplies, and even decide who to hire. Guided by general policies and coached instead of being directed, such teams are highly motivated to cut costs and increase productivity and quality, since their pay depends on improvement."[9]

These individuals and teams have been empowered to make decisions that once were within the sole purview of management. Parker describes three steps that managers can take to ensure that empowerment works and is practical for a given organization:

- *Develop goals, principles, and process understanding.* All employees need to know their work unit's goals and objectives so they can make informed decisions about how to accomplish them. In addition, they need a set of principles to guide those decisions, and they need to be educated about the entire business process so they can understand the effect on others of the decisions they make.

- *Provide training and education.* An uneducated work force cannot be empowered to make decisions, and untrained employees cannot handle responsibility. Formal training ensures that an employee understands his or her job thoroughly—not just how to do it, but what it means in terms of the whole organization. Moreover, cross-training in different jobs adds depth and insight to an employee's performance on the job.

- *Provide frequent, routine feedback on employees' performance.* If data flow only uphill from employees via management to top leadership, the people who actually do the work have no information on how that work fits into and affects the organization as a whole.

9. Ibid.

Parker compares the situation to the police having radar guns but cars not having speedometers: an unfair and confusing situation.

Daryl Conner disagrees with this generally accepted way to look at empowerment: "When someone has been assigned the right to make his or her own decisions, it is more appropriate to call this 'delegation.' The term 'empowerment' should be reserved for those situations where employees are not granted permission to take action on their own, but instead are asked to provide input to management as decisions are being made. You are empowered when you are valuable enough to others to influence their decisions—not when you are allowed to make your own."[10]

COMMUNICATING EFFECTIVELY ABOUT CHANGE

When the Orange County, Florida, Corrections Division embarked on major administrative and procedural changes, the director, Tom Allison, said that he met in small groups with every one of the 1500 employees in the division. "It took me about six months, doing it in two-hour increments, but I wanted all of them to hear from me personally what it was that I wanted us to do and how I wanted us to be."[11]

An organization that contemplates change but does not communicate those intentions to its employees is dooming itself, if not to outright failure, at least to a difficult change process. Secrets in a business organization tend to create an atmosphere of anger, tension, and resentment, all of which eventually result in poor function. In order to avoid rumors, lack of trust, and the perception that the company is engaging in "secret" (which is always read as "nefarious") activities, good communication about the process must be planned early on. Employees who are well informed about how the planned

---

10. Conner, op. cit., p. 195.
11. Tom Allison, director, Orange County Corrections Division, Orlando, Fla., interview.

changes will affect them, their work groups, and the company as a whole will accept the changes more readily. (See Exhibit 4.2.)

In addition to telling employees about the why and how of corporate change, it is effective for management to give employees regular feedback about the process of the planned changes. "Periodic progress reports, additional information incorporated within the management information system, conducting brief celebratory events when a change milestone is reached, are examples of how to monitor progress and, more important, ways to provide organizational members with relevant feedback."[12]

Developing and monitoring an effective communication plan are usually priorities of change management consultants. According to Beckhard and Pritchard, "The amount of effort that can successfully be put into communication is often underestimated. As well as providing people with information, communication is an essential prerequisite to changing attitudes and behavior, ways of work, relationships, and so on, all of which are likely to be necessary to fundamental change."

They define passive communication as the technique most often used to inform employees about proposed changes. Passive communication works one way only—downward—and rarely results in employee emotional commitment. In addition, passively conveyed messages may not be understood. Beckhard and Pritchard stress that "finding some way of measuring the gap between the messages sent by top management and those received by the intended audience is critical in an effective change process."[13]

Active communication, on the other hand, is designed to personally involve everyone in the messages that flow both from the top down and back up to the leadership. The pro-

---

12. W. Warner Burke, *Organization Development: A Normative View* (Reading, Mass., Addison-Wesley, 1987), p. 123.

13. Beckhard and Pritchard, op. cit., p. 86.

Exhibit 4.2

GOOD COMMUNICATION AT BELL ATLANTIC

Until recently, Bell Atlantic had operated as a monopoly and thus had little or no incentive to respond to market-driven forces or to focus more intensely on the needs of its customers. John Gamba, senior vice president for corporate and human resources, reports that "that mode of business operation has been permanently altered by deregulation of the communications industry and, as a result, by the appearance of a wide variety of companies that provide the same services as Bell Atlantic for competitive prices."

Suddenly, Bell Atlantic has been faced with the necessity of competing for customers, which has meant, says Gamba, that the company has had to "create a 'psychological environment' in which all employees have to buy into and practice the behavior patterns required to win in a competitive marketplace. This has entailed a radical change. As part of its change management process, Bell Atlantic constantly informs all employees about changes that will take place—especially about how those changes affect them and how the changes, as well as the employees themselves, fit into the total corporate picture. In addition, face-to-face communications stress the importance of changes employees will have to make.

All employees are expected to focus on customer requirements, work together as part of a high-performance team, and behave as owners of the business. In fact, the company feels so strongly about this that it has given the new corporate culture a name: Bell Atlantic Way Behaviors. Expectations are communicated to everyone and are reinforced by training and also by means of posters with slogans that remind employees about desirable behaviors and attitudes.

Exhibit 4.2 (*Continued*)

One of the methods suggested by consultants entails: (1) having managers identify and describe the old way of doing things; and then (2) asking them if and how the old ways will be sufficient to deal with new circumstances—circumstances identified in advance and shown as part of a likely future scenario. With a skilled facilitator, the managers come to realize they must say good-bye to the old ways and develop new ones.

Managers at all levels are committed to motivating employees to exhibit required behaviors and to participate in the corporate change process. "Every effort is made to help employees engage in Bell Atlantic Behaviors," says Gamba. "But if, after a reasonable time and use of a variety of motivating tactics, they cannot or will not, then there must be meaningful consequences as reflected in performance appraisals, compensation, and even job retention."*

*John Gamba, senior vice president for corporate and human resources, Bell Atlantic, interview.

posed changes are more likely to be internalized, resulting in more people thinking about what the changes will mean to them personally.

ADAPTING TO CHANGE BY LEARNING

According to Edgar Schein, three basic types of learning can apply to the organizational change process: knowledge acquisition and insight, habit and skill learning, and emotional conditioning and learned anxiety.[14]

14. Edgar H. Schein, "How Can Organizations Learn Faster? The Challenge of Entering the Green Room," *Sloan Management Review* (Vol. 34, No. 2), pp. 85–92.

Insight is difficult to achieve, says Schein, because it occurs only if a learner recognizes a problem. It does not guarantee a change in behavior, and there is no way to know whether knowledge gained by insight is cognitively valid. The acquisition of habits studied by the behaviorist B. F. Skinner is based on the creation of rewards and incentives to attain the desired behavior. The learning acquired here is slow because it requires much practice and a willingness to make many errors and be "temporarily incompetent," according to Schein. It is thus less than practical in business settings.

Emotional conditioning and learned anxiety are usually associated with Pavlov and his dogs waiting anxiously for dinner at the sound of a bell. Emotionally conditioned learning is based on reward and punishment, the latter of which is far more stable than the former. (Schein cites experiments in which dogs were forced into a green room by means of electrical shocks.) For example, "If employees have been through several traumatic reorganizations that involve downsizing or other painful events, they may come to treat all proposed change programs or reorganizations as bells that signal once again that they are being forced into a green room."

Schein explains that the anxiety of change can be managed by creating a different type of anxiety. That is, employees must come to believe that the current ways of doing things are no longer working and—even more important—they must connect this information with something they care about. "They must discover that if they do not learn something new, they will either fail to meet some of their important ideals, which will make them feel guilty, or they will put their job or security in jeopardy, which will make them feel anxious."

Schein says that three separate processes are involved in this type of learning:

- One type of anxiety (Anxiety 1) must be present in order to avoid immediate bad experiences.

- A different type of anxiety (Anxiety 2) must be introduced through disconfirmation, that is, the knowledge that things must change to avoid being placed in jeopardy.
- Anxiety 2 must be greater than Anxiety 1 in order to motivate action.

It is important to provide psychological safety during this process, in the form of encouragement, support, and coaching. If people do not feel safe, they will be unable to change and/or learn new habits. In a psychologically safe environment, in addition to support and encouragement, there are opportunities for training and practice, rewards for efforts in the right direction, and norms that legitimize making errors during the course of learning.

This process is far from easy, says Schein. It requires time, allocation of resources, and organizational leaders who can "overcome their own cultural assumptions and perceive new ways of doing things and new contexts in which to do them. They must acknowledge and deal with their own Anxiety 1 before they can appreciate and deal with the anxieties of others."

REWARDS, RECOGNITION, AND ACCOUNTABILITY

Of the major change that Bell Atlantic has undergone in the last decade, John Gamba says, "we are adamant about the fact that corporate change is an absolute requirement if the company is to survive and be successful. We are extremely serious about the need for all employees to buy into the new corporate culture and to participate in the change process."[15]

Bell Atlantic employees are given many opportunities to make the required changes, and they are provided with the tools to do so. If they do, there is appropriate acknowledgment, appraisal recognition, and compensation treatment.

15. Gamba interview.

As every parent knows, rewarding good behavior and making a child accountable for inappropriate behavior work—if the system is consistent and fair. The same principles hold true for organizations. During a period of organizational change, a company's reward structure should be linked to achievement of the goals mandated by the change. The policies and procedures for rewards and censures must be made known to all employees at all levels, and must be implemented fairly and impartially.

LAYOFFS AND REDUCTIONS IN FORCE

To employees of an organization, global competition, the company's future, censure and rewards, or their particular slot in the hierarchy pale when it comes to downsizing, the ultimate work issue. Despite all the literature on the subject, the devastating psychological consequences of downsizing are not entirely grasped. What we do know is that whether because of economic reasons, higher technology, change of leadership, or takeover and buyout, all organizations are in the midst of downsizing, often in successive waves, and the work force is responding negatively. Despite all precautions, individual workers tend, when laid off, to view the event as a personal failure.

When a substantial number of employees are let go, anxiety and discontent ripple through the ranks. Grief and fear are probably the two most dominant feelings accompanying a major lowering of the number of people who work for an organization. The consequence is often a significant morale problem. And when morale is low, production and efficiency suffer.

Thus, for reasons of both altruism and practicality, it behooves an organization's leadership to make reductions in force as anxiety-free as possible—for the people losing their jobs and for the employees who remain. (See Exhibit 4.3.)

The workers who lose their jobs are obviously faced with a major loss and a devastating crisis in their lives. No matter how positively a company handles letting an employee go, and

Exhibit 4.3

THE PHH APPROACH

PHH Vehicle Management Service's approach to staffing issues in redesigning, including staff reductions, was comprehensive. It included:

- Communicating honestly and often with the work force about the realistic potential for changes in the business to mean loss of jobs. Leaders also explained how employees could improve their chances of staying on by embracing the change, getting involved, learning new skills, and learning more about opportunities throughout the organization.

- Taking an analytic approach to identifying which employees to release during the downsizing that resulted from streamlining processes. Specific, written criteria were developed for determining who would succeed in the new roles—rather than merely allowing department, seniority, or any other categoric standard to be the basis of choice.

- Helping people find other jobs, both in different parts of PHH and outside the organization. People who left also got an outplacement package.

- Providing support for those who remained. Managers talked directly with employees who survived streamlining about the issues they faced during the transition, and they continued to communicate openly about additional changes and their potential impact on personnel status.

---

even if another job is immediately around the corner, the loss of employment is a huge blow to one's self-esteem. People do not recover from it easily, and the older one is, the more difficult it is to recover.

Exhibit 4.3 (*Continued*)

As a result, staffing changes have helped, not hindered, the momentum of change. In fact, the response of current staff has been largely positive. Lynn Berberich, vice president for human resources, attributes this partly to their communication and counseling efforts, and partly to the appropriateness of their staffing decisions. "Employees themselves believed we chose the right people for the new roles and let the right people go. This perspective helped them feel more positive about the changes."

From the employee's perspective, having the right skills to perform in the new environment is as important to job security as it is to job satisfaction; from the employer's perspective, it's fundamental to having the job done well. In addition to specific technical skills that may be required, teamwork skills are critical to the successful introduction of team work groups. "Effective teams cannot be developed overnight," notes Lynn Berberich. "We did a lot of training and coaching to help people understand the stages of teams, team styles, and effective team behaviors. We also provide ongoing support. Overall, it can take from three to five years to make the transition to a cohesive, productive team."*

*Lynn Berberich, vice president for human resources, PHH Vehicle Management Service, interview.

The people left behind in the office suffer from survivors' guilt and are also afraid for their own job security with, as a result, increased anxiety and decreased loyalty to the company.

In dealing with these employees, a large or midsize company with an employee assistance program can make confidential counseling services available. A smaller company can engage in the same process, albeit in a less formal and professional way. This is the function of the human resources department as well as management.

In addition, management should make a special effort to reaffirm its commitment to the employees who remain by providing positive reinforcement about their work, making certain that an increased workload is distributed fairly and that training and education are provided as needed, and engaging in active listening to the suggestions and complaints about the newly restructured work environment.

With care, the transition from desk or assembly line to unemployment line can be made less devastating. The first rule is for management to provide as much advance notice as possible that an employee's job is on the line. In addition, a company can provide job counseling and/or outplacement services, or it can enter into an agreement with a valuable former employee to provide occasional consulting services.

Other steps that management can take to ease the way for those whose jobs have been eliminated include:

- Making an effort to find other places in the organization for valued employees
- Retraining employees for other types of work within the organization
- Using former employees as temporary workers whenever the need arises
- Developing early retirement packages for long-time employees
- Providing severance packages as generous as possible and continuing essential benefits, such as health insurance, for an extended period

Salomon Brothers took a radically different approach to instilling the values they needed to make change successful: They moved their Product Support Organization from New York City to Tampa, Florida, and hired mostly new staff, taking only 20 percent of the employees from their New York headquarters. This "from scratch" approach allowed the organization to start with the values it needed—with no traditional mindsets to fight. Said Marc Sternfeld, managing director, U.S. Operations, "From the first day [that we knew we were going to move], we had to build a climate of trust. We told everyone, `We don't know exactly where we're going, but we're moving. About 125 of you will have jobs in the new place and 500 won't. We'll let you know in the next six weeks who will be in which category.'"

Sternfeld said instead of making a large general announcement, the company had private conversations with all employees to describe what was going to happen to them and why. "From the get-go, communicating to everyone was very important."[16]

In summary, communicating to everyone affected by a change is a necessary, but not wholly sufficient, step in assisting in the human change process. Widely disseminating information *is* critical to success, but equally critical are ensuring that communication flows easily among those affected by the change and developing employees as stakeholders and owners of the change process. True understanding of the human change process requires a change in management and, subsequently, employee behavior and attitude. The ultimate goal is substantial: to continuously enhance individual and organizational resilience and to manage successive change with increasing effectiveness.

16. Marc Sternfeld, managing director, U.S. Operations, Salomon Brothers, interview.

MOTIVATING AND ENABLING CHANGE

You have to understand corporate goals and what the proposed changes will attempt to accomplish, recognize the obligation to align your team to manage the changes, develop a specific plan, including task assignments and target dates, find an easy way to measure progress, and adopt a philosophy and practice of personal identification with and involvement in the change plan.

JOHN GAMBA, BELL ATLANTIC

Two and a half years ago, the United States corporation Corning Glass and the Mexican glass manufacturer Vitro began a joint-venture business alliance. Julio Escamez, a Vitro executive, offered this toast: "Vitro and Corning share a customer-oriented philosophy and remarkably similar corporate cultures."

In practice, however, the cultures clashed radically in almost every way. Vitro executives felt their Corning counterparts were too direct, too willing to focus on problems, and moved too fast. Corning managers chafed at waiting for important decisions about marketing and sales because in the Vitro culture only top managers could make these decisions and they were busy with other matters. Vitro's sales approach was less aggressive than Corning's. Corning's lunch-at-the-desk, home-by-dinner schedule and Vitro's long lunch times and late closings made arranging meetings a heroic venture.

With no advance plan for aligning cultural factors in both companies with desired new operating behaviors, integrating the two organizations proved impossible. In February 1994, Corning returned Vitro's $130 million contribution to the venture, and the two companies agreed to dissolve the alliance.[1]

---

1. A. DePalma, "It Takes More Than a Visa to Do Business in Mexico," *The New York Times* (June 26, 1994), p. 5.

A large city government organization instituted an activity-based management system and gave departments volumes of cost data relating to their tasks. Financial officers were surprised when few field supervisors changed the way they did business or reduced their costs based on the new information. Then they realized no one was using the data as a management tool because they didn't have the job skills to understand its purposes or how to apply it. The departments also were unaware of the city's broader strategic objectives, which the change to activity-based management was designed to support.

An electronics equipment manufacturer changed from a revenue-based performance measurement system to a profit-based one in order to eliminate the large discounts that the company's biggest customers traditionally had received. Compensation for account executives, however, continued to be tied to revenue—and management saw no reduction in discount levels. When planners revised the system to link executive compensation to profits, account executives lost no time in embracing the vision. Discount levels fell from 29 percent to 20 percent off the list price within a couple of weeks.[2]

Each of these examples reflects a common way in which organizations set themselves up to fail in introducing change: overlooking powerful factors within the company or agency that drive and underlie behavior—and that can either make or break the desired outcome. Exhibit 5.1 enumerates key organizational factors and represents their role in the change dynamic.

ASSESSING ORGANIZATIONAL FACTORS

W. Warner Burke says that organizational behavior is more like waves and interconnections than entities or events.[3] Jeanie Daniel Duck compares it to a mobile: When change

2. G. Hall et al., "How to Make Reengineering Really Work," *Harvard Business Review* (November/December 1993), pp. 119–133.

3. W. Warner Burke, "The Changing World of Organization Change," *Consulting Psychology Journal* (Winter 1993), pp. 9–17.

Exhibit 5.1

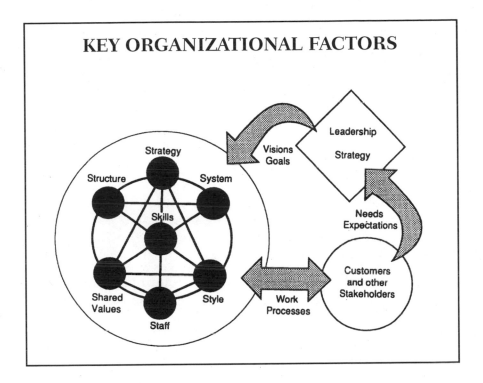

moves one part of the mobile, change management realigns the other parts to keep the mobile in balance.[4] Whatever analogy is used, the goal in addressing organizational factors is ensuring that every factor that can affect organizational behavior is designed or redesigned to support the change.

STRATEGY

An organization's strategy is both a starting point for change and a reference point for continuity. Any change an organization undertakes should be based on and congruent with its

4. J. Duck, "Managing Change: The Art of Balancing," *Harvard Business Review* (November/December 1993), pp. 109–118.

strategy. Sometimes the need for change becomes clear as a result of strategic planning—goals cannot be achieved without making changes. In other cases, the organization realizes the need to improve, but strategic planning helps decide what to change. For example, leaders at PHH Vehicle Management Services recognized that increasingly aggressive competition from companies like General Electric required PHH to continue to do more for customers to remain an industry leader. Based on a thorough strategic assessment, leadership chose business process redesign as part of the framework to achieve PHH's strategic goals.

For organizations that plan change within the context of an existing strategy, it is critical to revisit the plan periodically in light of the changes made and ask:

- What new elements of strategy are required to support the desired change (e.g., increased emphasis on marketing, supplier alliances, outsourcing)?
- How well do other activities in the strategy fit with the planned changes?
- How will new ways of doing business affect current business plans?

It is also important to assess how well other organizational factors support the strategy. Edgar Schein tells the story of several companies whose shared values made their strategy impossible to implement. In one case a company had become successful by developing and selling products that were "important to society." When their strategy called for diversifying into products that were less high-minded, some managers felt the whole concept went against the company's core values. On a practical level, selling the new products required marketing skills and expenditures the company had not previously needed. Developing this capacity would have taken some resources away from research and development for the "meaningful" products—and top leaders would not make that trade-off. As a result, the new strategy never had a chance to succeed.

Dunlop Tire avoided this potential clash of organizational factors and desired new behaviors. The company conducted a formal assessment of how well its organizational factors supported its strategic goals of developing a process focus based on special customer groups. They identified one critical mismatch—a functional, rather than process-based, communications network—and realigned communications to support the new approach before the old system could subvert new goals.

It is also important to avoid confusing the strategy with the change. For example, PHH Vehicle Management Services President Bill Adler emphasizes that business process redesign is *not* the company's strategy; it is a means to the company's chosen ends. By maintaining this perspective, it is possible to monitor the effectiveness of organizational change in accomplishing strategic goals. This direction and coherence constitute a critical foundation for all change management initiatives.

STRUCTURE

In many organizations structural change happens all the time. At Citibank it was called the "annual reorganization."[5] Often, the impact on employees or the way work gets done is minimal. (One employee compared being reorganized into a new department with changing homerooms: same work, different home base.)

Meaningful restructuring, however, is strategy-driven and integral to a broader change vision. In many cases, structural change is the dominant change around which all the other organizational factors must be aligned. Today, common trends in structural change include moving from the traditional hierarchical model to a flatter organization and organizing by process instead of function (even when a process includes workers from different sites around the world).

In managing structural factors in change, it is important to

---

5. W. Warner Burke, *The Burke-Litwin Model: Master Class,* participant manual, 1994.

pay attention both to the formal organization chart and to the critical elements in the white space: who reports to whom, where the real power lies, and how the work actually gets done. (See Exhibit 5.2.)

Exhibit 5.2

COMMUNICATION PLANNING: THE NETMAP SYSTEM

How to communicate information is as important as what to communicate. Before planning a strategy for communicating about a change, it is important to evaluate current communication policies, vehicles, and tools. One instrument for such assessment is Coopers & Lybrand's Netmap System, a computerized technique for diagramming existing communications networks, working relationships, and previous organizational success in communicating through existing channels.

The Netmap System helps organizations visualize and manage both internal and external communications networks with stakeholders affected by the change. The assessment includes questioning staff systematically on their regular communication patterns (formal and informal, static and interactive) and cross-referencing the answers to produce communication maps.

Netmap's communication maps facilitate communication activities with identified constituent groups. In addition, the system answers questions such as these, which provide information critical to organizations managing change:

- Are planned business strategies being carried out in practice?
- Who is consulted on key issues?

Exhibit 5.2 (*Continued*)

- How important are particular individuals in the functioning of the grapevine?
- What happens to communication patterns when organizations change their structure?
- Are messages—whatever the form—being passed on effectively?
- Who is in regular contact with the organization's customers?
- Where do people need to be physically located under the change?

In assessing how the new structure will affect the organization and its ability to change, it is important to ask:

- How will the organization chart need to change to align with the process changes proposed?
- How should reporting structures change?
- What power structures will change as a result of new groupings? What will replace them?
- How will employees get the work done? Individually? In teams?
- Should the physical layout of work spaces change?

At Salomon Brothers, Inc., the Product Support Organization completely reengineered its structure around cross-functional teams with the goal of eliminating process variance. Marc Sternfeld, managing director, U.S. Operations, calls their attention to making structural factors support the change a "sociotechnical" redesign.

"We believe in teams, so everything has to line up," Sternfeld says. "The competition lines up with the facility, which lines up with the way the furniture is designed, which lines up with how people are hired. The furniture has low barriers, so you have a job family of about 10 people facing each other with a conversation pit in the middle with swivel chairs. That facilitates high performance, because you have people who are doing similar jobs as part of the team all being able to see and talk to each other as opposed to cubicles...which are lined up like soldiers on the march."[6]

Another important aspect of structure to consider is geography. Most large organizations today have many far-flung sites, often around the world. Geographic dispersion can affect an organization's willingness and ability to change in many ways. One example is international quality standards.

The basic model for this quality practices assessment is the Malcolm Baldrige Award. Established in 1987, the intent of the award was to spur U.S. industries to catch up in an international quality race. Other countries and regions have also adopted the Baldrige award; however, culture clashes can occur in various areas and operation. For instance, the Baldrige quality criteria, considered "too American" by the Europeans, have had to be tempered by the ISO 9000 sets of guidelines to become acceptable.

Otis Elevator, a subsidiary of United Technologies, Inc., operates internationally to sell, manufacture, distribute, and service its products and administer its operations. Its corporate divisions and strategic business units (SBUs) use a self-assessment audit. The adoption of quality self-audits is a managerial change designed to give a worldwide corporation a comprehensive, common, universally recognized set of criteria for excellence. (See Exhibit 5.3.) Because it also requires participants to adopt desirable quality management activities and behaviors, it helps to reinforce the new ways of operating and to foster continuous development.

When, driven by market requirements for ISO 9000 certification, some European-based operating units worried there might be a conflict between this standard and the Baldrige award, both Otis and Carrier, another subsidiary of United

---

6. Marc Sternfeld, managing director, U.S. Operations, Salomon Brothers, interview.

Exhibit 5.3

DIFFERENCES IN CULTURE

Otis is a worldwide, decentralized corporation. A decision implemented at the corporate level does not necessarily involve the rest of the company. The culture also varies in different individual business units. Change management actions that have helped with the independent cultures have gone beyond training designed to promote the quality survey instruments, analyzing barriers to quality and translating the audit document into many languages. One consultant who was a project manager, says, "In international corporations, attention to domestic issues, such as translation, helps make people become more comfortable with the change."

Culture doesn't only define the mindset of organizations but goes beyond to national characteristics. Companies doing business abroad may find they have differences, not only of language and of style, but of basic assumptions about the host country. It is culturally important to observe and understand difference in approaches. When a product is defective on a Japanese assembly line, the people in charge will stop the line to see where the mistake occurs; the American assembly line will keep running while technicians look at the product to find out why it is defective.

Technologies, Inc., responded with training that showed that, despite a few philosophical differences, ISO standards and the assessment criteria complement each other. Otis was among the first companies to use this process internationally—in seven languages in 50 countries on five continents.

At AlliedSignal, the geographic challenge for change planners was introducing cycle time reduction in dozens of manufacturing plants in three product sectors from New Jersey to

Exhibit 5.3 (*Continued*)

A recent Conference Board survey shows a contrast between manufacturing and service respondents from U.S. and Europe-based companies. European companies and Europe-based firms count as a change management success the shift in their leadership style. One reason may be that change at the top, though not necessarily linked to a change management strategy, occurred earlier in U.S. companies such as Xerox and General Electric, whereas in Europe, with the emergence of a new generation of charismatic managers who dominate the multinational scene, the change has been more spectacular. The survey quotes a *Fortune* article exploring the "startling change in European business culture," which cuts across all European industry.

Culture, or "the way of doing things," can also be a factor of growth when one is willing to look at the experience of others and benefit from it. At Thermos, the leadership operates according to the Japanese principle of spending enough time in the planning and definition stage to avoid time-consuming changes during the engineering and manufacturing phases.*

*Brian Dumaine, "Payoff from the New Management," *Fortune* (December 1993), pp. 103–110.

Hong Kong. Fine-tuned scheduling helped introduce the initiative quickly and virtually simultaneously; a standardized workshop approach kept the information consistent. Adopting common process definitions and common measurement standards also created a shared framework while allowing the flexibility individual differences required.

Change management experience teaches that when it comes to a showdown between the current culture and the change objectives, the culture always wins. In an organization's culture, values are one of the most important aspects and a key driver of individual and group behavior. An important step in change management is understanding what the organization's values are, whether they will support or hinder the change, and what needs to be done to motivate and create real values change. Here are some of the questions it's important to answer in planning for change management, perhaps with the help of a formal organizational values assessment:

- What new beliefs about the organization/department/unit will be necessary to make the change?
- What values do employees hold now?
- What paradigms or traditions will be broken or built as a result of the change?
- How will employees know or understand new goals and expectations?
- How will individuals or groups be rewarded and recognized for successfully making the change? What will happen if they do not/cannot change?
- What incentives, intrinsic or extrinsic, will be used to drive new behaviors? What other steps will be taken to create new behaviors that indirectly reinforce the new values?

SHARED VALUES

Although aligning organizational values to support change is essential to success, values are difficult to manipulate. In some organizations, consistent values trace back to the organization's founder as enduring principles. In other instances, organizations begin a change process with several sets of conflicting values to address, as a result of values differences among various subcultures within the broader group.

In addition to focusing on values that support the change, organizations need to look at people's values about change itself. The organization's history of introducing other changes can have a significant effect on how people react to a current change. If previous changes were unsuccessful and people "rode them out," they may attempt the same strategy this time. If previous changes have been successful but frequent and intense, people may be burnt out by the pace of change and unwilling to get on board again.

While communicating new values is a necessary step in promoting their adoption, it is never a sufficient step. As one employee responded in a cultural assessment survey, "We see the company's values every day on our coffee mugs. Their importance is we got new mugs."

Instead of simply announcing values, the key is providing opportunities and incentives for employees to live them. When this is done continuously over the long term, new behaviors can bring about a gradual change in values.

The experience of Prudential Direct, a new operation of Prudential designed to market insurance and other financial services to consumers through nontraditional means, illustrates many of the values-related issues in change management. Explains Quality Director Doug Nelson, "Our parent corporation, Prudential, is nearly 120 years old, and perhaps one of the more conservative companies in a very conservative industry. The culture of the industry is to be risk-averse and cautious, moving carefully, not making mistakes. At Prudential Direct, we have to be more like other direct marketers. This means we have to create a fast-acting, responsive, and dynamic organization, a real entrepreneurial business that is totally focused on the customer. Among other things, this requires a flatter organizational hierarchy than Prudential's has been, and Prudential Direct has to be more team-based."[7]

To support the change, Prudential Direct leaders began by developing a values statement as the basis for creating shared values around the new business goals. Values developed include: trustworthiness, customer focus, respect for each other, and winning. The new company has used a number of communication vehicles, including memos, meetings, and personal visits with managers to explain the values and the vision for change. An employee orientation program, Stepping

---

7. Doug Nelson, director of quality, Prudential Direct, interview.

Stones (for current and new employees), outlines the new ways of doing business and explains how people will now be evaluated and rewarded.

Perhaps the most difficult value to promote has been the concept of teamwork. Although teams had been used previously in Prudential's backroom operations, they were not common among frontline staff. Many key personnel had been hired for their technical expertise, and most had worked independently with no need for managerial or team skills. People realized that the impact on their daily lives could be revolutionary; some had little confidence that teams would do the job better than experts working on their own, and others felt inadequate in their team behavior.

After providing training in team skills to every employee, Prudential Direct began working on getting senior management to model the new values and behaviors. Because they, too, were used to operating in the old style, they needed coaching to understand what specific actions they needed to take to support the change.

The Prudential Direct change management efforts are continuing, as those trained in team behaviors are now getting the opportunities to put the new skills to work on the job. In summing up the experience to date, Doug Nelson notes some important pluses and minuses. "First, top management has been very supportive. Second, we have an enthusiastic, receptive staff of associates (employees, as opposed to middle managers). We are selling what they want to buy. [But] we tend to understand how to do this team-based thing with people who are doing repetitive types of tasks. It is a lot harder with people whose primary work is ideas, marketing, etc. You can't just pull a bunch of books off the shelf and 'sheep-dip' people in the new way of operating."[8]

Organizational experts differ about the extent to which strong, entrenched values and culture *can* be changed. Daryl Conner says that those who believe it's impossible are those

8. Nelson interview.

who have tried and failed.[9] Edgar Schein points out that organizational values include deep assumptions and superficial assumptions. In some cases, changing the superficial ones (which is easier) may be enough to make a change succeed. In addition, sometimes an organization can harness strong values in support of change even when they seem to contradict the change. Schein gives the example of a company whose strong belief in individual turf and vertical communication and authority was an initial barrier to developing lateral communication and a process orientation. Ultimately, however, they developed ways to retain the value and work together as the new approach demanded.[10]

In Coopers & Lybrand's experience, values and culture *can* be changed, although it takes at least three years to see new values begin to develop. It is also clear that every change effort does not require a major values shift. The key is assessing the gap between current and desired values. Where old values will seriously obstruct change or new values are essential for working effectively, values are a necessary and legitimate target for change management. In the short term, assessing values can also help set priorities among changes; it is wise to start first on projects without major values concerns.

STAFF AND SKILLS

As organizations change, staff issues are always fundamental, with skills an inseparable concern. Questions to answer include:

- What knowledge, skills, or abilities will employees need to have to make and sustain the change? How will staff obtain them?

9. Daryl R. Conner, *Managing at the Speed of Change* (New York: Villard Books, 1993), op. cit.

10. Edgar Schein, *Organization Culture and Leadership* (San Francisco: Jossey-Bass, 1991), pp. 1–358.

- What tasks will employees perform in the new workplac
- How will jobs or job groupings differ from current patterns?
- Will workloads increase or decrease? How will they be allocated?
- Will the type of staff, educational levels, or skills mix of employees need to change?
- What new behaviors will be needed?
- Will employee autonomy and flexibility increase or decrease?
- How will the staff implications of downsizing be dealt with?
- Are work force diversity issues relevant?

Staff issues have several clear implications for action. Training, as discussed in Chap. 4, is an important way in which organizations motivate and enable staff to support change, both by creating new programs and by integrating new elements into existing programs.

At AlliedSignal, Inc., CEO Larry Bossidy felt he had to go even farther than training to support the goal of becoming a world-class company. He worked personally with the human resources department to develop a whole new approach to recruiting staff for positions, both internally and externally. The company also restructured traditional career paths.

Bill Adler, president of PHH Vehicle Management Services, placed a similar premium on having the very best people on his reengineering team. He involved the company's top performers, regardless of their department affiliations, and he didn't hesitate to replace managers who weren't contributing with people who could make things happen. The incredible growth and learning that reengineering team members experienced allowed many people in the organization to move up in responsibilities much more rapidly than they could have under the old system—a benefit of change that organizations often overlook in the throes of staffing upheaval.

Manufacturing company Owens-Illinois's reengineering effort also included training in teamwork, but it identified other skills the work force would need to support the change. The company offered a variety of training workshops on topics such as effective meeting management, time management, conflict resolution, performance management, and intergroup dynamics.

Companies that are, or want to be, international in scope are finding that global brains can be an important staff asset. GE, which is moving aggressively into markets in China, India, and Mexico, is trying to create a cadre of executives with international savvy. In some cases, companies are training in-house staff in new languages; in others, they are actively recruiting new managers who have international experience and perspectives.[11] Many European companies already have many different nationalities in their management and work force, which can be an important asset for globalization.

MANAGEMENT STYLE

When British Airways was privatized, the demands of competition drove widespread changes in the organization. One factor alone—emphasizing a customer orientation in addition to the traditional safety/engineering focus—had enormous implications for the way managers led and managed in the new operation. To prepare them to put everything in customer terms, managers went to the baggage claims area at Heathrow Airport and talked to passengers picking up their luggage. These visits helped them put customer service reports into personal perspective, and eventually many managers could be seen regularly around the area helping customers with their luggage and engaging them in conversation. Perhaps the ultimate modeling of a customer-oriented management style occurred when British Air's CEO had himself bumped off the Concorde when his flight was overbooked.[12] The new managerial style in Europe, however, has made a strong shift from its

11. T. Smart, "GE's Brave New World," *BusinessWeek* (November 8, 1993), p. 64.
12. W. Warner Burke, *The Burke-Litwin Model.*

earlier easygoing, collegial manner to a more assertive and creative one.

Under CEO Noel Goutard, Valeo, a French vehicle parts maker, last year increased profits by 26 percent. Ask anyone in the company how, and "'Quality, service, price,' comes the answer" writes Paul Hofheinz. "Goutard has so effectively conveyed these buzzwords from the top to the bottom of his organization that even the farthest-flung outer-office secretary sounds like Peter Drucker."[13] Goutard says that if he has bought factories in Korea, Brazil, Mexico, and Turkey, it isn't to cut costs but to have access to these fast-growing markets.

The need for change is felt all across European industry. In 1987, the Swedish ASEA and the Swiss Brown Boveri, two sedate European engineering companies, merged to become ABB, a competitive machine that is one of the most important players on the global scene and often cited as an example of European success. ABB chairman, Percy Barnevik, is a master at extreme downsizing. The result is that headquarters staff has shrunk from 4000 to 200. In mid-1993, ABB underwent its second major restructuring since the 1987 merger. It created superregional groups to address regional markets in Europe, the Americas, and Asia, and folded several of its industrial divisions. Firms such as ABB are becoming masters at reengineering, TQM, and other management trends in favor in the U.S., but with a far more important focus on the supply side. Barnevik strongly believes in obtaining lower costs from the suppliers. Where ABB differs from other firms is that it helps suppliers come up with solutions for bringing down costs. It also uses supplier feedback for new products, often providing parameters and asking suppliers to come up with their own design. One Japanese supplier, asked to create a new version of a product, came up with one 30 percent cheaper than the new version. Roland Andersson, a purchaser for

13. Paul Hofheinz, "Europe's Tough New Managers," *Fortune* (September 6, 1993), pp. 111–116.

ABB, says, "Our first reaction was to get angry and ask, 'Why didn't you do this before?' They said, 'Because you didn't ask.'"[14]

The most common need managers face in change initiatives today is learning how to manage an empowered work force in a leaner organization. At U.S. West Communications, for example, workers have responsibility for redesigning the organization and its work processes, and the work force is being reduced by 50 percent with the active involvement of the union. For managers accustomed to traditional, hierarchical management roles (and an adversarial union-employer relationship), adapting to the new environment requires a 180-degree turn. A combination of training, coaching, and changes in performance management and rewards is helping the transition to occur.

In addressing issues of management style, answering the following questions is important:

- What will managers' new roles and responsibilities be?
- What observable behaviors will managers be expected to display?
- What will the relationship between managers and employees be? Team leader? Coach? Inspector?
- What new skills or abilities will managers need? Delegation? Communication? Employee development?
- How will managers develop new skills and perspectives?
- How will managers be measured and rewarded for making the change?

Changing styles can be painful and difficult for managers, particularly when the flatter organizations they now work in result from mandated downsizing. The commissioner of the U.S. Bureau of Reclamation, Daniel P. Beard, is familiar with this scenario; his agency was one of the first to support U.S.

---

14. Ibid.

Vice President Gore's "reinventing government" initiative, which will ultimately reduce staff by 25 to 30 percent in some areas. Beard chose a novel way to show his support for managers in the Denver office who are making efforts to be less bureaucratic and more innovative and to live with a manager-employee ratio that has gone from 1:5 to 1:15 on average. He hands out "forgiveness coupons" that read, "It is easier to get forgiveness than permission." Recognizing that the bureau has traditionally been a control-oriented organization, he tells managers, "If you do something bold and innovative and it's controversial and people start yelling at you, then you whip this sucker out and wave it, and then they have to shut up....You have protection."[15]

SYSTEMS

An organization's systems include a variety of mechanisms intended to support people in accomplishing their work and the company/agency's mission. They include the communications network and information system, the performance measurement and rewards system, and others, such as the organization's policies and procedures and the budgetary/resource allocation process.

COMMUNICATIONS NETWORKS/INFORMATION SYSTEMS.   Wanda Orlikowski of the Sloan School of Management calls information technology a "social artifact," whose designers consciously or implicitly incorporate their assumptions about how work should be done, what the division of labor should be, and how much independence and responsibility individual employees should have."[16] When these assumptions match an organization's current goals and vision, the information system can support the appropriate work behaviors. However, as

15. S. Barr, "Bureau Concedes Downsizing Pain," *The Washington Post* (April 14, 1994), p. A29.

16. W. Orlikowski and D. Gash, "Changing Frames: Towards an Understanding of Information Technology and Organizational Change," paper submitted to the 1991 Academy of Management Meeting (January, 1991).

J. Pfaffenberger points out: "Once [information systems are] created...the opportunity for social choice diminishes. An implemented technology carries with it a powerful vision of the society in which it is to be used, replete with an equally powerful endowment of symbolic meaning, and sometimes an obligatory plan for the way people will have to arrange themselves to use it."[17]

In our experience, changes in information technology produce lasting competitive advantage only when they are part of, and complement, broader, process-oriented change. Sometimes it is the availability of technology that enables process change, decentralized operations, and moving responsibility further down in the organization. In other instances, new cross-functional or transnational cooperation requires new—and newly compatible—information architectures.

Because information systems play so critical a role in today's environment, no organization can afford to overlook this factor in planning for change. While this makes common sense, two barriers can make information technology difficult to deal with. The first is the time and expense involved in revamping existing systems. In the Naval Industrial Improvement Program, for example, leadership instituted centralized coordination of previously autonomous naval ordnance stations. Each had its own information system(s), and none was compatible with the others. Some had only recently installed or upgraded their systems at considerable expense. The cross-functional teams that worked on redesigning an umbrella system found that differences in the way work was done and managed complicated defining common system needs. Yet meaningful performance measurement required common reporting. They found it was possible to overcome these problems, but it required commitment, time, and resources.

The second barrier relates to turf issues, compounded in this case by the technical nature of information systems.

---

17. J. Pfaffenberger, *Microcomputer Applications in Qualitative Research* (Newbury Park, Calif.: Sage Publications, 1988).

Sometimes information technology people are isolated from the change process and, in return, refuse to cooperate in redesigning a matching information system (or are unable to cooperate, because key decisions have already been made that tie their hands). In other cases, the lack of a common language and goals among operations and information people gets in the way of creating a supportive system. In addition, some managers don't understand information technology and have a hard time reacting to concepts and monitoring applications. The best way to overcome this barrier is to make information technology (IT) an active partner in planning, managing, and implementing the change.

The process followed in the redesign of Banca di America e di Italia (BAI) illustrates the value of paying the right kind of attention to information technology issues. In a total redesign of each banking transaction (e.g., check deposit, savings withdrawal), the IT team's mandate was to develop a new approach to storing the data on each redesigned transaction with the maximum level of detail. Current system limitations had no influence on the new design. In building the IT system, the team worked closely with operational management and with the people who would be using the new system, such as tellers and branch managers. The system was put into place gradually, as each transaction redesign was completed; staff were given substantial training on how to use the system prior to its introduction. With a well-fit system in place, BAI has been able to open 50 new branches without any increase in personnel and little new systems expense, and revenue has doubled in the five years following its introduction.[18]

In addition to the formal information system, organizations also have communications networks (formal or informal) that reflect the way people get internal information. Understanding this factor is critical in communicating effectively about the change. About half the firms recently surveyed by The Conference Board said they have done a formal communica-

18. G. Hall et al., op. cit.

tions audit as part of change initiatives to be sure they understand how employees receive information, how they would prefer to receive it, and how effective internal communications networks really are.

PERFORMANCE MEASUREMENT/REWARD SYSTEMS.   Performance measurement includes defining and evaluating performance and giving feedback to employees. Rewards include raises in salary, bonuses, stock awards, perquisites, and promotions. W. Warner Burke believes these are the most important systems factors to address in change management, because they have the most influence on individual behavior.[19] Chairman and CEO of the Xerox Corporation, Paul Allaire, agrees. "One of the things I learned a long time ago is that if you talk about change and then leave the reward and recognition system exactly the same, nothing changes," Allaire told the *Harvard Business Review*. "And for good reason: people quite rationally say, 'I hear what he is saying, but it's not what I get paid to do or what I get promoted for. So what's in it for me?'"[20]

At Xerox, the measurement/rewards system has been completely redesigned to align individual compensation with the strategic objectives of the company. It rewards good performance and penalizes poor performance of the individual, his or her division, and the corporation. If you get a good individual performance rating but your unit or the company has had a bad year, your bonus won't be as high. The way performance is measured has also changed radically to drive new behaviors. People used to be judged on a scale of five, and good performers usually got fours and fives. Now the system rates on a seven-point scale, and top people often get twos and threes on some specific criteria. The goal of the painful new approach is to promote continuous individual improvement and to increase the overall quality of the work force. "We're not doing it just to be perverse," Allaire explains. "It's hard for any orga-

---

19. W. Warner Burke, *The Burke-Litwin Model.*

20. "The CEO as Organizational Architect: an Interview with Xerox's Paul Allaire," *Harvard Business Review* (September/October 1992), p. 106.

nization to get out of its history. We have to be very diligent, so that old habits, practices, and behaviors don't sneak back in."[21]

At General Electric, the worldwide corporation has moved to a team structure, and the senior management groups consist of managers with multiple competencies rather than one specialty. While the senior team allocates resources and provides coordination, teams complete day-to-day activities without management input or oversight. To create allegiance to a process, rather than to a boss, General Electric has restructured its performance appraisal system as "360-degree appraisal routines." This term conveys the range of people who rate each manager and employee: peers, superiors, and those who work under them. In addition, people are paid for the skills they develop, not for the work they perform.[22]

Experts today differ about the extent to which rewards and incentives have succeeded in producing desired outcomes. We suggest that when they do not, it is usually because an organization is rewarding the wrong behavior or a behavior planners did not foresee. A simple example is the case of Imri Airfreight, which was trying to decrease the number of packages that were damaged in transit. The solution: offering incentives to the frontline staff to find damaged packages. This story is a prime example of what one author called, "The Folly of Rewarding A When You Wanted B."[23]

It is also important to note that performance measurement and reward systems may not need to be completely redesigned for every change. In many cases, organizations have added new criteria to those that already exist to help stimulate new desired behaviors while retaining others that are still worthwhile.

21. Ibid.

22. J. Byrne, "The Horizontal Corporation: It's about Managing Across, Not Up and Down," *BusinessWeek* (December 20, 1993), p. 76.

23. W. Warner Burke, *The Burke-Litwin Model*.

OTHER SYSTEMS FACTORS.   Although information and performance measurement systems have the most obvious impact on an organization's willingness and ability to change, other factors can also either promote or hinder a new way of working. In France, for example, Valeo now creates a new budget every six months instead of once a year, so that the company can adjust its strategy more rapidly; the old budget system was too slow for the newly innovative manufacturer. At New York State Electric and Gas, developing a new, process-based financial system not only responded to an increased process focus but also created additional organizational changes (increasing accountability, changing management practices, and increasing individual responsibility for process improvements) that had to be addressed and managed. Similarly, as the United States works to "reinvent government" into an organization that works better and costs less, a key systems element being considered is the adoption of activity-based financial systems. This policy is critical, because under the previous aggregate budget system, government departments had little information that tied specific costs to particular activities.

In addition, an organization's policies and procedures (both formal and informal—"the way we really do things around here") can be a silent, but formidable barrier to change. For example, a policy requiring multiple sign-offs or elaborate paperwork can stop a cycle time reduction initiative before it starts. Prudential Direct's Doug Nelson believes another common business practice—midstream budget cuts—can be anathema to change. "In order to have an effective and valid change management program, senior management must recognize the longer-term nature of the initiative and commit to a funding approach consistent with that view. This is not a process that readily lends itself to putting the pedal to the floor and then cutting off the gas supply, even if the intent is to accelerate it again later. Constancy is very important," Nelson says.[24]

24. Nelson interview.

The systems and policies in every organization will vary. The key is to include these factors in an assessment of change readiness and revamp them as needed to support the new environment. The following are some of the questions it is important to ask about systems:

- What information will be available for people to make effective business decisions?
- What expectations will exist for people to be able to make and act on information? What tools?
- What level and types of performance are expected? How should performance be measured to align with new directions?
- How will new information or measurement systems be integrated with existing systems?
- What other systems barriers could hinder change (financial systems, policies and procedures, inadequate or inappropriate internal communications networks)?

PUTTING IT ALL TOGETHER

How do organizations "put it all together" and line up each organizational factor squarely on the side of change?

The experience of The Equitable, one of the top five U.S. insurance corporations, is a good example of managing multiple factors to create organizational support for change. Using a new strategy for remaining competitive in a turbulent, diversifying market, The Equitable made a variety of fundamental structural changes in the 1980s. These included converting its internal real estate operation to an independent company with 16 subsidiaries and affiliates, creating new companies for individual and small business customers, and carrying out large-scale decentralizing of many functions. From the outset, senior management planned for complementary changes in internal reporting relationships, allocation of resources, departmental structures, and shifts in decision-making authority to lower levels of management. They also provided extensive training to develop required new job skills and teamwork-oriented management styles; linked all staff training/development programs to evolving Equitable strategies; and created mechanisms to select the best staff for new strategic goals and reward them appropriately.

Managing issues related to shared values also received a great deal of time and attention. The decentralization and the new strategy for aggressive competition required the company to overturn its conservative values and develop a shared orientation toward risk taking, innovation, closeness to customers, more open communication, and a greater sensitivity to markets and profits. To promote the new values, The Equitable sponsored an aggressive program to communicate them to the work force. The company also conducted a survey of employees to determine their attitudes toward work, the company, and management. The results of the survey helped leadership understand the gaps between current and desired values and what was needed to bridge them—needs largely met through communication and training. As follow-up surveys showed the new values taking hold, The Equitable provided many opportunities for reinforcement over time.[25]

Motivating and enabling change are critical factors in any change effort. Each relates to the need to understand the drivers of both individual and organizational behavior. As drivers of behavior are understood, actions can be planned and executed to leverage behavior in the desired direction. Motivating and enabling individuals is complex work. Viewing organizations as systems is a convenient, helpful framework for balancing the varied, and often competing, changes required in behavior.

25. K. Dechant, "The Complex Task of Culture Change at The Equitable," *A Manager's Guide to Corporate Culture* (New York: The Conference Board, 1989).

BECOMING AN EFFECTIVE CHANGE LEADER

I personally have to be the lighthouse to make sure we're moving toward the team-culture direction....I'm the one who doesn't move off the vision principles....I have to make sure we keep moving in the right direction and look for signs, talk to people, and see how they operate, watch their performance....You could not do this in place....The only way we had a chance was by disorienting everybody completely, changing their titles, changing their state, changing what they do. MARC STERNFELD, SALOMON BROTHERS, INC.

LEADERSHIP FOR CHANGE: CARDINAL, NOT OPTIONAL

Becoming an effective leader for change is perhaps the most important thing executives can do—for their personal development and for the companies they direct. A recently reported study in the *Harvard Business Review* quantifies our empiric experience: Without continuous, committed, active leadership, organizational change does not succeed. The study reported the association between the actual monetary outcomes of business process redesign efforts, their anticipated impact, and the degree of top management commitment in the projects. In both European and U.S. examples, companies with high management commitment met or exceeded anticipated financial goals; those with low management commitment had lower yields; and all fell substantially short of anticipated monetary benefits.[1]

---

1. G. Hall et al., "How to Make Reengineering Really Work," *Harvard Business Review* (November/December, 1993), pp. 119–133.

John Kotter says producing change is the primary function of leadership.[2] He and others distinguish between leadership and management. For example, good managers plan deductively and produce orderly results, while leaders set direction and develop vision and strategies; managers organize and staff activities, while leaders align people by communicating the vision and empowering action.[3]

In practice, of course, one executive can be both a leader and a manager. Because both types of skills and qualities are critical to effecting change, executives who are more "leader" than "manager" can develop a management team that reflects both. Harold Sperlich, a top member of Lee Iacocca's management team at Chrysler, describes the symbiosis this way:

> The dramatic leadership that Iacocca provided was in the classic leadership mode—a guy you believe in, you'd follow into battle. He was so strong that, at the worst time, knowing his hand was on the helm, a dealer would keep his money in the business; a supplier would bankroll us...a guy would come over from Ford....[He] provides leadership in battle, his fundamentals are right, and he behaves consistently....My own leadership style is a little bit like his, but on a smaller scale. I'm not big enough, and I'm not supposed to be....I'm more actively involved in trying to promote results through common goals and an enabling style....But as chairman and CEO, he's got to establish the fundamental values.[4]

2. John Kotter, *A Force for Change: How Leadership Differs from Management* (New York: The Free Press, 1990).

3. John Kotter, "What Leaders Really Do," *Harvard Business Review* (May/June, 1990), pp. 103–111.

4. W. Warner Burke, "Conversations with Harold K. Sperlich," *Organizational Dynamics* (Vol. 12, No. 4, 1984), pp. 13–36.

CHANGE LEADERSHIP BEHAVIORS: WHAT EFFECTIVE LEADERS DO

Management theorist Abraham Zaleznik believes that leaders are born, not made. This may be true in the sense that not every CEO can duplicate the charisma of Lee Iacocca. However, effective change leaders exhibit a range of behaviors that any executive can adopt, that every management team of a changing organization should have—collectively, if not in every individual—and that organizations can foster as they "grow" managers. This section discusses critical change leadership behaviors. (See Exhibit 6.1.)

EMBRACING CHANGE WHEN IT'S NEEDED

Jack Welch summed up the leader's need to be open to change: "Change before you have to."[5] Executives cannot lead for change until they have committed to it themselves. Taking

---

5. Stratford Sherman and Noel M. Tichy, *Control Your Destiny or Someone Else Will* (New York. Doubleday, 1993).

Exhibit 6.1

WHAT EFFECTIVE CHANGE LEADERS DO

- Embrace change when it's needed
- Develop a vision for change
- Communicate
- Shake things up
- Stay actively involved; walk the talk
- Direct and review change management planning and implementation

this step involves much more than analyzing projections and giving lip service to innovations. Once the mind has accepted the need for change, the heart and soul must follow.

Just as middle managers and employees may resist change, many top executives may find that change is difficult to accept, much less to drive. In some cases, change may mean rejecting the very foundations on which an executive's past success has been built. Personality, experience, turf, and the many other reasons human beings cling to the status quo may equally apply.

It is also clear that change, at least in the short run, is often painful, and the vision of what change may do to the organization can be a major obstacle on the road to commitment. At Premier Bank, for example, Chairman and CEO G. Lee Griffin led a successful business process redesign project that reduced the costs of the core processes of the bank by approximately 20 percent, upgraded its technology significantly, enabled it to enhance customer service by quantum leaps, and positioned it for tremendous growth in its markets. But in committing to the project, Griffin felt the pain of downsizing, a pain that was doubly sharp because previous, smaller-scale improvement efforts had produced some success—but not enough to meet current company goals.

"I have been here since 1962, and I know the people," Griffin recalls. "The employees who were affected [by downsizing] were, in many cases, people who were older, had been here the longest, and had a lot of loyalty....I had to make the decision to do this knowing that it would adversely affect morale. We had been through a lot, some real tough times. But we [had] turned things around, and over the last few years we had been doing very well, and the employees took pride in what we had accomplished. I knew this [new change] would bust their balloon. And at the end of the project, I knew that many people would say that senior management does not care about loyalty and hard work."[6]

---

6. G. Lee Griffin, chairman and CEO, Premier Bank, interview.

Jim Eibel of Ameritech, who is leading the change from monopoly protection to competition in his company, notes another reason it can be hard for executives to embrace change. "Today I know that once we've positioned ourselves as a competitive company this job—my job—won't exist any more," he explains. "I just hope my name will still be on a box somewhere in the organization chart." How does Eibel deal with the stresses and the ambiguities? "I've had some sleepless nights. You have some tough things to do....It's important that you really do believe in it, that you're fully committed to the necessity for change."[7]

For many top executives, it is the CEO or one of their peers who helps them understand the reason for the change and develop the commitment. For CEOs or other top corporate executives, however, recognizing the need for change and the conviction to lead despite obstacles must come from within.

If the risks of necessary change seem great, consider the alternatives. Commenting on the compelling need for aggressiveness and innovation in European businesses, Marco Tronchetti, managing director of Pirelli Tire Company, noted, "The power of Japan cannot be fought by doing business in Europe as usual. We have to fight as if we were starting from scratch." Rhône-Poulenc's Michel de Rosen, an executive in the throes of privatization, has watched CEO replacements occur at Carrefour, Thomson Consumer Electronics, and the Paribas financial group. He pointed to a need to embrace necessary change that is even closer to home. "In the past, an advanced degree from the right school was enough....Now, performance counts for much more."[8]

---

7. J. Huey, "Managing in the Midst of Chaos," *Fortune* (April 5, 1993), pp. 38–48.

8. Paul Hofheinz, "Europe's Tough New Managers," *Fortune* (September 6, 1993), pp. 111–116.

DEVELOPING A VISION FOR THE NEW ORGANIZATION

The day that Larry Bossidy became CEO of AlliedSignal, Inc., a company forecast came out predicting a negative cash flow of $435 million by the end of 1991 and of $336 million in 1992. Debt was 42 percent of capital, and surveys showed that executive morale was lower than the company's bottom line.

Change was clearly needed, but envisioning its direction and the shape of things to come could only come from the leadership. Bossidy began by setting aggressive goals for performance on a variety of measures: 6 percent annual gains in productivity; operating profit gain of 4.3 percent for 1991–1994; working capital turnover gain of 4.2 to 5.2 times per year; and a gain in return on equity of 7.5 percent by 1994.

Bossidy also worked with AlliedSignal's top 12 executives to develop the company's "to-be" vision. (See Exhibit 6.2.) Committing the company to "strive to be the best in the world," the vision specifies a customer focus, teamwork, innovation, and speed as key means to the end. The vision also specifies that AlliedSignal will become a "total quality company by continuously improving all our work processes to satisfy our internal and external customers." The definition of a total quality company includes: (1) producing satisfied customers; (2) focusing on continuous improvement; and (3) having highly motivated and well-trained employees. It also includes taking high-quality steps to achieve excellent business results, such as managing by fact, taking a process orientation, and using a business planning process that has quality goals, steps to achieve them, and the means to measure them.

This example illustrates a critical change management activity that only top executives can perform: developing a vision of the new organization. No one else has the power to set overall direction. In fact, vision is considered the key to leadership.[9]

9. John Kotter, op. cit.

Exhibit 6.2

VISION STATEMENT: ALLIEDSIGNAL

Our vision	We will be one of the world's premier companies, distinctive and successful in everything we do.
Our commitment	We will become a total quality company by continuously improving all our work processes to satisfy our internal and external customers.
Our values	**Customers.** Our first priority is to satisfy customers.
	Integrity. We are committed to the highest level of ethical conduct wherever we operate. We obey all laws, produce safe products, protect the environment, and are socially responsible.
	People. We help our fellow employees improve their skills, encourage them to take risks, treat them fairly, and recognize their accomplishments, stimulating them to approach their jobs with passion and commitment.
	Teamwork. We build trust and worldwide teamwork with open, candid communications up and down and across our organization. We share technologies and best practices, and team with our suppliers and customers.
	Speed. We focus on speed for competitive advantage. We simplify processes and compress cycle times.
	Innovation. We accept change as the rule, not the exception, and drive it by encouraging creativity and striving for technical leadership.
	Performance. We encourage high expectations, set ambitious goals, and meet our financial and other commitments. We strive to be the best in the world.

A vision is a picture of the future, a common goal that sets direction and around which everyone can rally. The most effective visions are simple, clear, and compelling; they challenge the organization to take great strides, but they also serve the interests of key constituencies. Paul Hebert, the former COO of Corsair Marine, notes the importance of developing visions that are relevant and associated with the leader who developed it. "People do need to have a vision of what is to be, but it has to be presented in real life out on the shop floor," Hebert says. "You've got to be out on the floor presenting it, getting to know your workers, reinforcing today what you said yesterday. That's how your workers gain confidence in you, the leader."[10]

Roy Bauer, writing about IBM's Silverlake project, says that a leader envisions possibilities others don't.[11] Yet this requirement does not mean that "born visionary" is part of the leader's job description. Larry Bossidy learned the power of quality improvement tools while he was a vice president at General Electric, and he brought this knowledge and experience to AlliedSignal. At the simplest level, a leader may see possibilities that others don't because it is his or her job to look for them.

From one perspective, developing a future vision is a task that managers can prepare themselves for, arrive at using factual analysis, and get help in formatting effectively. But IBM CEO Lou Gerstner's reflections show that it is also a risky enterprise that requires courage and confidence to carry through. "There are no recipes," he says of IBM's new focus on the marketplace, execution, and teamwork, the hallmarks of his vision of how IBM can recover lost market strength. "There are no certainties that what I'm doing is going to work. You've got to go on instinct."[12]

10. Paul Hebert, former COO, Corsair Marine, interview.

11. Roy Bauer et al., *The Silverlake Project: Transformation at IBM* (New York: Oxford University Press, 1992).

12. S. Lohr, "On the Road with Chairman Lou," *The New York Times* (June 26, 1994), pp. 1, 6.

COMMUNICATING THE CRITICAL NEED FOR CHANGE, THE CHANGE VISION, WHAT CHANGE WILL COST IN HUMAN TERMS, AND RESULTS AS THEY OCCUR

Chapter 4 discussed the importance of communication in overcoming resistance to change and promoting organizational buy-in. While organizational communications overall are critical in change management, change leaders at all levels must take an active role in communicating about change. The visible involvement of top leaders in itself shows that the organization is taking this change seriously—and so should its employees, stakeholders, and customers.

Change can be more readily accepted when there is a compelling need for it. So one focus of change leader communication must be on the urgency of working differently, even when the change itself involves pain. In fact, Coopers & Lybrand consultants' experience suggests that major change never occurs successfully unless the need for change is obvious and the situation prompting the need is serious and fundamental—when a company is losing market share, no longer shows a profit, is going through a merger, or wants to expand globally.

At PHH Vehicle Management Services, President Bill Adler made communicating about the company's business process redesign a top priority for himself and the top executives in the reengineering steering group. He articulated the urgency of changing while the company was still a market leader. Aggressive new competitors had already reengineered in an effort to achieve market dominance. Adler championed the change in employee forums, written communications, and with his own management team. "Bill took the time needed to build consensus," recalls Lynn Berberich, vice president for human resources and an active participant in managing the change to a process-focused company. "During steering committee meetings, the top management team was encouraged to air all the issues and problems they had. Often, the same issues came up repeatedly, especially around the controversial issue of where each process began and ended which affected traditional turf boundaries. But Bill gave everyone time to feel their concerns had been heard and addressed, meanwhile using team skills to move people toward consensus."[13]

Jim Prebil, who heads the BPR effort at PHH and devotes full time to making change happen, has also been actively involved in communicating about the change. Notes Lynn Berberich, "Jim does everything that Bill does, and he also speaks as an advocate for change in a variety of situations. He is so enthusiastic about the improvements we're making that he does a great job of motivating others. He has also cleared the way for changes by addressing policy- and culture-related obstacles head on in his discussions with people.

"When the need for downsizing resulted from process redesigns, Bill and the entire senior management team led honest and open discussions of the probable impact of BPR on the work force and how individuals could help themselves during the transition. As positive results of reengineered processes have occurred, Jim and Bill have been personally involved in letting everyone know about successes, from employees to customers."[14]

IBM CEO Louis V. Gerstner believes that selling the new IBM culture to the worldwide enterprise is a fundamental aspect of his job. Since becoming CEO in 1993, he has traveled extensively to talk to IBM workers and customers. At first, outlining the critical need for IBM to become more productive, he announced plans to cut costs by $7 billion through streamlining. Then he made the rounds to present his strategies for responding to the technological shift away from IBM's traditional mainframe and minicomputer businesses and helping IBM maintain its revenues. Stage three has been to personally champion culture changes he feels are critical to strategic success. In one typical week, Gerstner's schedule

13. Lynn Berberich, vice president for human resources, PHH Vehicle Management Services, interview.
14. Ibid.

included trips to Atlanta, Georgia; Orlando, Florida; and Helsinki, Finland, to explain and promote the new ways of doing business.

Gerstner believes changes must be sold by the chief executive face-to-face. "It's not something you do by writing memos," he says. "You've got to appeal to people's emotions. They've got to buy in with their hearts and their bellies, not just their minds."[15] Although some executives are more comfortable and skilled at communication than others, making the effort is important regardless of the leader's personal style. If top managers don't explain and promote the change, their silence communicates volumes of the wrong message to the organization.

Leaders, of course, take risks in associating themselves with change. AT&T's Glen Hazard, the reengineering team leader for the Global Business Communications Systems unit, expressed a concern natural for an 11-year veteran of the organization. "I did not want to be the crusader who never came back from the crusades," he said. As others on the management team began wavering when they saw how radical the redesign really was, Hazard made a total commitment to the change. He recognized that it was critical to communicate a strong and unwavering commitment, even if the leaders themselves faced uncertainties.[16]

Not only do leaders need to give their total commitment to the change, but they need to assume full responsibility for its results. One of the least pleasant traits of the corporate culture is that the shift-the-blame game is played at every level. What distinguishes true leaders is their capacity for accepting accountability for the success or the failure of any project they initiate, from small adjustments to major process redesign.

15. S. Lohr, op. cit.
16. G. Hall, op. cit.

SHAKING THINGS UP

It is axiomatic that maintaining the status quo neither promotes nor energizes change. Effective change leaders show that change is real by changing not just the rudiments of the organization but also its routine.

At the U.S. Department of Energy, for example, Secretary Hazel O'Leary recognized the need to change the paradigm of the organization after she was appointed to the position by President Clinton. As a starting point, she introduced carefully designed chaos into the system to change people's perspectives and attitudes. For example, the agency had been accustomed to a hierarchical structure and top-down initiatives. To energize and showcase change, O'Leary called in about 20 subject specialists in areas such as information technology, nuclear energy, and fossil energy. She directed them to review the issues for six months and tell her what the department should be doing in these areas.

For the first two months, the people involved talked among themselves, wondering "What does she want?" "What are we supposed to do?" Then they used their own initiative and got to work. Not only did the strategy get everyone's attention, it was also the first step toward creating an empowered team culture in the department.

Leaders can also shake things up by challenging traditional thinking and decisions and by giving others permission and encouragement to do the same. At PHH Vehicle Management Services, innovative thinking was critical to successful process redesign. Yet the PHH culture emphasized loyalty and supportiveness; confrontation, especially in the form of challenges to authority, was stringently avoided. The senior management team began promoting constructive confrontation by practicing it and asking other managers to do the same. Not everyone responded positively to the approach. However, Lynn Berberich notes a clear correlation between units' success in implementing BPR and the degree to which the unit adopted the new, challenging style.

Heralding change by doing things differently does not

require total organizational deconstruction to succeed. One of Larry Bossidy's strategies at AlliedSignal was to introduce small but focal changes to the routine. For example, managers began using the language of total quality management to discuss issues, prompting employees to do the same. Soon everyone was framing issues in terms such as "process variation," "finding root causes," and "doing it right the first time."

In a similar way, the organization began holding meetings according to TQM-style ground rules. Shaking things up at the basic, everyday level, meant that people couldn't miss the fact that things were operating differently now, and it was unthinkable not to go along.

STAYING ACTIVELY INVOLVED, WALKING THE TALK

This behavior separates the real change leaders, those who truly enable the change, from the figureheads who simply support it. Because top executives have so many responsibilities, it would be easier if their job in leading change were over once the change vision was articulated and accepted. In fact, however, successful change management requires their continued, priority support as champions, role models, and overseers of change. Their active involvement may include activities as diverse as chairing or participating in a steering committee, presiding over awards ceremonies celebrating employee participation and success, regularly reviewing measurement indicators to assess the progress of change, taking a central role in ongoing decisions relating to the change, continuing to communicate in large forums and small, and visibly adopting any new behaviors other managers or staff need to adopt (e.g., displaying a more participative management style, focusing on processes and objective data in decision making, or behaving in accordance with new company values).

For actively involved change leaders, walking the talk is both a long-term and an everyday activity. Fortunately, this aspect of leadership demands more focus and commitment than time.

For example, when the Aluminum Company of America

(ALCOA) adopted a set of values (integrity, safety and health, quality of work, treatment of people, accountability, and profitability), the new chairman, Paul O'Neill, took the first step in demonstrating corporate integrity. Before accepting the traditional perk of membership in a nationally known golf club, O'Neill asked whether women and blacks were accepted as members. Because they were not, he refused to join—and ensured that ALCOA would no longer pay for anyone else's dues there or at any facility where discrimination was in force.[17]

In the city of Indianapolis, Indiana, walking the talk meant that the mayor had to have the courage of his convictions, even when the change hurt members of his own political party. Mayor Stephen Goldsmith came to office with a mandate to improve city services and cut costs, in part by having city departments compete for jobs with private industry. Street repair employees told Goldsmith they could cut costs and outbid industry, but only if he would cut their overhead by firing many of the patronage employees who "supervised" their work. Despite the ire of his local party chiefs, Goldsmith dismissed more than half of the political appointees.[18]

At PHH Vehicle Management Services, a focus on teamwork has required managers be more coach than boss. The senior management team has provided a model by serving as mentors to those adopting the new behaviors. The phrase "walking the talk" might have been invented by Larry Bossidy, whose personal insistence on aggressive goals and speed has set the standard at AlliedSignal. *Fortune* magazine reported that when his handpicked vice president of quality and productivity laid out a five-year plan, Bossidy told him to do it in two years—and to be prepared to close his office in three years to take an operations job. "This obvious commitment at

---

17. L. Stepp, "In Search of Ethics," *The Washington Post* (March 31, 1991), pp. H1, H4.

18. D. Broder, "Mayor Shows Gore's Team the Way," *The Washington Post* (August 25, 1993), p. A19.

the top gave all of us a sense of personal urgency about making the changes," notes one AlliedSignal executive.[19]

DIRECTING CHANGE MANAGEMENT PLANNING AND IMPLEMENTATION

While following these principles, effective change leaders also direct and review other formal change management planning and implementation activities. This role complements their direction of the technical aspects of the change. Just as top management's support for and involvement in the change itself sends a message to the organization, so their knowledgeable leadership of change management activities prompts and reinforces organizational attention to the human and systems dimensions of change. Thus, an effective change leader leads both change *and* change management.

ORGANIZING LEADERSHIP FOR CHANGE MANAGEMENT: ROLES AND STRUCTURES

Beyond effective change leadership skills, successful change management efforts define specific roles for change leaders and develop a change leadership infrastructure to support and facilitate change implementation throughout the organization.

IDENTIFYING THE RIGHT PLAYERS, COVERING ALL THE POSITIONS

During the adoption of change, people in an organization play four key roles (see Chap. 7). These four key roles are those of change sponsors, change agents, change advocates, and change targets. While only a select few are change sponsors, change agents, and change advocates, everyone who works

---

19. T. Stewart, "AlliedSignal's Turnaround Blitz," *Fortune* (November 13, 1992), pp. 72–76.

under the new system is a change target. In fact, change sponsors, agents, and advocates are all change targets before they become supporters. In addition, change sponsorship includes two roles: initiating sponsor and sustaining sponsor. Initiating sponsors have the power to start the change process (e.g., chairmen or CEO-level leaders, or top executive steering groups they assemble). Sustaining sponsors maintain the change process because they have the closest proximity to the change targets (e.g., process, function, or department managers, SBU leaders, general managers). Both sponsorship roles are critical, and both should remain actively involved throughout the change process.

The success of the change depends on all change management roles being known and understood by each player and on leadership roles being assigned to the right people and played effectively. Problems at any level can thwart the desired outcome.

One of the most common problems in making a change is incorrectly identifying and generating effective sponsorship. Not only must sponsors support the change; they also need the power to make change happen. (See Exhibit 6.3.) Too often, however, organizations motivate a variety of enthusiastic change advocates to support the change, but don't focus enough attention on getting the systems' power brokers on board.

Based on eight case studies that Robin Cooper and Robert Kaplan conducted in industry, they concluded that failure of an organization to implement a change to activity-based management (ABM) is most likely to occur:

- When the initial change sponsor fails to identify sustaining change sponsors for the implementation phase of the project (when people must begin to use the information to make improvements); and/or

- When the change sponsor fails to identify the targets of change, with the result that the people who ultimately must use ABM information are not involved early enough in the

Exhibit 6.3

CHARACTERISTICS OF AN EFFECTIVE CHANGE SPONSOR

CHARACTERISTICS	DEFINITION
Power	The organizational power to legitimize the change with the targets
Pain	A personal stake in making the change succeed, to the extent that the current situation is more painful/costly than the change
Vision	A total, in-depth understanding of what change must occur and the effect the change will have on the organization
Public role	The willingness and ability to demonstrate commitment to and active public support for the change
Private role	The willingness and ability to meet privately with agents to discuss progress, problems, and concerns with the change target
Performance management	The willingness and ability to reward desired behaviors and confront undesirable behaviors regarding the change
Sacrifice	The commitment to pursue the change despite personal or political prices that may be paid

process to buy into the change. They also don't learn to understand and use the system as it's being developed, guaranteeing at best a lag time between implementation and application.[20]

Sponsorship for change is so critical that the effectiveness of sponsors should be regularly assessed. If they don't have the commitment, the power, or the ability to fulfill the role, they should be replaced, and quickly.

---

20. R. Cooper et al., *Implementing Activity-Based Cost Management: Moving from Analysis to Action* (Montvale, N.J.: Institute of Management Accountants, 1992).

It is also important to remember that, while roles frequently overlap, sponsorship cannot be delegated to change agents. Change agents may be from the quality staff, the human resources department, or another department. Their power to make change happen is usually limited to a subprocess.

Developing an Effective Infrastructure: Linking Key Players

Effective change management also needs an infrastructure that cascades change leadership roles throughout the organization and links each level of leadership to the others. A formal change management infrastructure:

- Avoids what Daryl Conner calls "black holes" in change sponsorship: areas of the organization with no intermediate link from the initiating sponsor to the change targets.[21] In this scenario, for example, employees may be trained in TQM skills and recognize that the CEO espouses total quality values. But in departments or units with no sustaining sponsor, no one ever uses TQM approaches on the job. When middle managers or supervisors are change advocates, although they can *help* TQM happen, they cannot *make* it happen because they have no legitimizing authority. They can't reward those who use the approaches, they can't secure additional training in statistical process control, and they can't cross turf lines to give teams time and authority to meet.

- Motivates change by starting at the top; each successive level sees that those above are already on board.

- Enables change by providing "point guards" at each level who have the defined responsibility—and the authority—to look for and solve problems that get in the way of change

---

21. Daryl R. Conner, *Change Sponsorship Workbook* (Atlanta: ODR, 1992), pp. 36–42.

(e.g., organizational factors needing change, political issues, turf issues).

- Reinforces and helps maintain the change. Formally defined roles and structure institutionalize the change; the infrastructure is part of "the way we do business."

Exhibit 6.4 shows the leadership infrastructure that AlliedSignal is using to manage its cycle time reduction initiative, total quality through speed (TQS). This initiative also

Exhibit 6.4

ALLIEDSIGNAL'S TQS INFRASTRUCTURE

Steering Group Corporate-wide Each SBU	Who: Top corporate leadership Roles: Ensuring training; identifying and overcoming barriers; monitoring results; rewarding teams and managers; communicating about TQS
Process Champions (only featured in EMS TQS initiative) One for each core business process in each sector	Who: Senior sector-level managers Roles: Advocate TQS, model management behavior, allocate resources; change policies to overcome barriers, monitor progress
Process Leaders One for each core business process at sector level and in each SBU	Who: SBU-level managers, "best and brightest" Roles: Work with process champions to resolve problems; serve as focal point for day-to-day TQS activities; work with SBU process leaders; identify best practices, opportunities (SBU-level); build support for TQS in SBU; monitor progress; lead improvement efforts; identify barriers and communicate with sector leader; chair SBU steering group

Exhibit 6.4 (*Continued*)

Team Champions One for each team	**Who:** SBU managers who often have responsibilities in process being changed **Role:** Liaison to process leaders; communicate needs for resources or resolution of problems; report on progress; help develop team charter; review team products and process; guide development and measurement of performance indicators
Team Facilitators One for each team	**Who:** Come from all levels and functions; receive special training **Roles:** Run team meetings; assist in use of TQS tools; help develop reports on findings; work with the team champion to overcome barriers, get personnel and resources

involves reengineering the corporation around core business processes in each of its three business sectors and each of the small business units (SBUs) within them.

The TQS infrastructure was designed to provide visibility and support for TQS efforts at critical points in the change process. It also showed the entire work force that some of the company's most senior managers were accountable for the success of TQS implementation. In the Engineered Materials Sector (EMS), for example, the president of the Fibers Division, the largest division of EMS, is the sector-level process champion for the Customer-Linked Commercialization process. The other two process champions include another division president and a sector vice president.

This support structure is comprehensive for each core business process, addresses long-term needs and facilitates interaction among SBUs.

THE ROLE OF CONSULTANTS

"If a team of people maps how you do your work, you may feel uncomfortable, but they'll show you how to do it a lot better and faster," says Larry Bossidy, CEO of AlliedSignal. Every change initiative needs the guidance of people who understand change management issues and have an effective implementation methodology. Some organizations have that expertise in house. At PHH Vehicle Management Services, for example, well-qualified internal staff were available to handle the change management aspects of the transformation, while Coopers & Lybrand provided support for the technical aspects of the company's business process redesign.

When organizations do not have internal change management expertise, they often engage consultants, who may train internal staff in change management principles and/or provide overall direction for change management planning and implementation. Sometimes, as occurred with changes to the machinery of government in Australia in 1987, insiders prepare a change management plan and ask a consultant to review it. Exhibit 6.5 describes some of the roles consultants often play in the change management process.

What cannot appear on a chart, however, is one important aspect of change management support that consultants provide: the fresh, objective, impartial outsider's perspective that companies frequently need. Consultants also provide the executive coaching and pushing that organizations often require. Another reason to bring in consultants when considering change or when an initiated change process stalls is the commitment, the renewed energy or boost, provided. An additional factor to consider is that consultants charge for their services, and an organization not wanting to throw money out of the window will work closely with consultants and perhaps pay more attention to their suggestions than those coming from the ranks of regular management or the work force.

When an organization decides to work with consultants, it is important to consider the following issues:

Exhibit 6.5

CHANGE MANAGEMENT: ROLES CONSULTANTS OFTEN PLAY

- Assessment, using tools and techniques to help organizations identify change management barriers, opportunities, and networks
- Training in change management principles and methodology or to meet special needs (e.g., helping managers adopt new styles, teaching teamwork skills, and developing change leadership)
- Planning for change management, using tailored workshops and planning processes
- Values and vision development assistance
- Infrastructure design and role development
- Assistance in redesigning organizational factors to support change, such as compensation and performance measurement systems, information systems, and financial systems
- Organizational communication planning and development
- Project management assistance

---

1. *When to bring consultants in.*   Because change management is integral to the change process, change management planning should begin as soon as change planning itself begins. If consultants are to play a major role in change management, this is the time to get them involved. As Chap. 7 details, initial change management assessments and planning are critical to facilitating change. Consultants are often brought in later in the process, when problems that have

already stalled change need to be corrected. This is a valid role, but a better approach is to get help to identify and solve potential problems before they occur.

2. *What characteristics to look for.*   At a minimum, change management consultants need knowledge of the issues and effective approaches in organizational change; experience with change management in the type of organization that needs their services and the type of change needed; and the time and staff capacity to provide all the services needed over the long term. Perhaps most critical, they should have a proven methodology for implementing change management; the "how-to" aspect is the heart of the matter. Approaches that are unidimensional (e.g., they help an organization assess potential resistance to change, but offer no organization-specific guidance in overcoming that resistance) simply don't work. Change management must be comprehensive and tailored to a particular situation, or it cannot succeed. It is also important to consider the specific qualities an organization may need, such as consultants with international experience.

3. *Whether to use the same consultants for the technical and the human aspects of the change.*   Organizations often use one firm to assist them with both the technical change and the change management process. As long as the consultants have sufficient expertise and personnel to provide both services well, this is an effective approach. Most important, it facilitates an integrated consideration of change and change management needs and avoids issues of coordination among consultant groups. However, when a firm lacks expertise or excellence in one of the areas, it is best to bring in someone else who has superior skills to cover that dimension. With proper coordination, multiple consultant groups can work together effectively.

4. *Whether to meet the experts before hiring their firm.*   A consulting firm's methodologies and reputation are important, but what an organization is really paying for is the expertise of the specific people who will work with it. It is useful to identify, meet, and review the credentials of those who will be there for effective assistance; the "guru" on the letterhead can't do much if he or she is not involved.

LEADERSHIP FOR ORGANIZATIONAL RESILIENCE

> Things are going to get tougher; the shakeouts will be more brutal, the pace of change more rapid. When we, some day in the future, look back on this sunny time in 1994, I hope it will be with the satisfaction of knowing we understood it for what it was—and used it to get ready for what was to come.
>
> *Jack Welch, CEO, General Electric, speaking to the Economic Club of Detroit, Michigan*[22]

> Only 25 percent of our products are sold in the developing world, where 80 percent of the population lives. I see growth possibilities everywhere.
>
> *Helmut Maucher, CEO, Nestlé*[23]

> We [European companies] have to go from being a tanker to a torpedo. Our way of life is at stake.
>
> *Marco Tronchetti, Managing Director, Pirelli*[24]

As already pointed out, many organizations today realize that the change they are now envisioning and enabling is just one of many to come. Management theorists have moved from talking about the management of change, to the management of surprise, to the capacity for faster and faster transformations.[25]

22. Jack Welch, "CEOs on the Economy: A Matter of Exchange Rates," *The Wall Street Journal* (June 21, 1994), p. A22.

23. P. Hofheinz, op. cit.

24. Ibid.

25. E. Schein, "How Can Organizations Learn Faster?" *Sloan Management Review* (Vol. 34, No. 2, Winter 1993), pp. 85–92.

While providing leadership for today's change is critical, anticipating and preparing for tomorrow's can be equally imperative. Few organizations to date have developed this kind of permanent resilience, so those that do have a significant competitive advantage.

How can executives lead for resilience? Three steps are key: preparing themselves, preparing new leaders, and preparing the organization. Leaders who develop and practice the change leadership behaviors discussed earlier are prepared to lead for resilience. The key is recognizing that the need for change is likely to be a constant and can be a positive dynamic force. PHH Vehicle Management Services has this kind of leadership. According to Lynn Berberich, "There is a clear recognition among senior managers that change is necessary to survival in the future. In the organization, some people still expect this [reengineering] period of change to end, but others realize it will be a constant in this company. [President] Bill Adler describes our environment as transformation."[26]

Adler and PHH have also taken steps to prepare new leaders to develop change leadership skills as a permanent organization capability. This perspective underlay their desire to handle change management themselves for their BPR project and to have Coopers & Lybrand consultants train their people to manage the technical aspects of BPR, rather than having long-term consultant involvement. When the company hires new staff or promotes from within, a proven ability to flourish and contribute in a changing environment is one of the selection criteria. They also offer many opportunities for managers at all levels to get involved in managing change, "home-growing" the skills they need for the future as more experienced leaders mentor their colleagues.

PHH is also addressing a critical leadership problem in developing organizational resilience: managing the pace of

---

26. Berberich interview.

change. "The fast pace at PHH has taken its toll," notes Lynn Berberich. "The people we've called on most during reengineering are at risk of burnout. They need a period of recovery, but we haven't had that luxury. In leading for resilience, we're trying to see and utilize the depth of our organization, so that more people can carry the load and to enhance organizational learning. This seems to be the best way to build a long-term capacity to handle change."[27]

The three types of preparation for resilience (current leaders, new leaders, the organization) also suggest a broader need that encompasses all three: the need for continuous learning. Leaders for resilience must constantly learn in order to overcome their own assumptions, go beyond their experience, and envision new ways to improve. Leaders for resilience can also develop learning organizations, which create opportunities for growth organization-wide. Resilient organizations will still face external threats and market forces they cannot predict. But they will also have the capability to respond to those forces rapidly and follow Jack Welch's sixth rule of change leadership: "Control your own destiny, or somebody else will."[28]

27. Berberich interview.
28. S. Sherman and N. Tichy, op. cit.

A COMPREHENSIVE CHANGE MANAGEMENT APPROACH

THE COOPERS & LYBRAND APPROACH TO CHANGE MANAGEMENT

Get outside help at the beginning. We struggled for a year before we recognized we needed help.

J. M. SHAFER, SOUTHWESTERN POWER ADMINISTRATION

For decades, profit, margin, and bottom line were the driving forces in business. With the increased competitiveness of our times, customer needs and expectations once again come to the fore. Critical consulting tasks involve helping the client organization to determine why the change to customer perspective is needed. Coopers & Lybrand makes customer perspective a key aspect of the process for making change manageable and sustainable within client organizations.

Change is a complex process, unique in every case. The corollary is that there can be no predetermined set of answers to managing change. Coopers & Lybrand's approach integrates not only widely recognized and effective theoretical principles from business, management, sociology, and behavioral psychology experts, but practical field experience acquired firsthand by working with clients from a broad variety of backgrounds in all types of situations, from complex to simple onetime interventions.

Our approach integrates conceptual models for analyzing and understanding the dynamics of complex organizational change with the tools and techniques appropriate to managing the change. Needless to say, the approach can be as varied as the number, type, and size of the organizations to which it is applied. There is no set method and no predetermined pattern of intervention. Rather, Coopers & Lybrand works with each individual client organization to help it travel from its "as is" stage to its desired goals.

A PLANNED APPROACH

Any organization with a planned approach to change has to address three critical factors:

1. Creating a vision of where it wants the organization to go and building people's commitment to that vision and the change that will bring it about
2. Mapping a strategy to make the business process change work
3. Providing an environment for continuous improvement to sustain the change

The key component in the Coopers & Lybrand management approach is a four-step change project management process. The project is not a change master plan but a way of getting started. It seeks to:

- Analyze the existing or "as is" condition
- Determine the change process best adapted to the organization's goals
- Reflect a valid conceptual framework for change
- Involve and empower people toward a shared vision

The four steps are as follows:

1. *Assessment.*   Analyzes the "as is" situation; defines the purpose and nature of change.
2. *Planning.*   Articulates and defines the entire change pro-

cess required to bridge the gap between "as is" and "to be" and defines tactical plans. Establishes the change structure on the basis of both human and technological parameters.

3. *Implementation.* Builds understanding and commitment to change; trains toward the new goals; establishes new ways of working.

4. *Renewal.* Supports culture change and work force empowerment; builds in measurement processes for change, including achievement and learning.

THE ASSESSMENT PHASE

- What is the compelling need for change?
- What are the guiding principles that will govern the change process?
- What are the key roles in the change process, and who is responsible and accountable for action?
- What is the history of change in the organization?
- What other change projects are ongoing within the organization?
- What is envisioned as the desired future state of the organization?
- What are the enabling strategies for achieving the vision of the future?
- What is the communication strategy for the change project?
- What are the requirements for redeployment of the work force?
- What is the level of awareness of change management issues within the work force?

These are some of the questions to ask in the assessment phase. This first step is a vital one in the change process. An organizational analysis incompletely conducted puts the entire change strategy and implementation in jeopardy.

The primary focus of the assessment phase is to determine

the organization's readiness for change and to assess levels of understanding, ownership, and commitment to change at all levels of the organization. The odds of successfully implementing change grow as the existing culture on one hand and the behaviors and assumptions required by the change initiative on the other are aligned. During the assessment phase, Coopers & Lybrand collects and analyzes information needed to understand the human aspects of a planned change, so that a sound change management strategy can be developed. It is also at this point that management can begin to win support for the change from various groups in the organization.

Useful assessment tools are existing conceptual models.

The Burke-Litwin Model of Organizational Performance

An empirically based model, Burke-Litwin classifies the social behavioral factors in influencing organizational performance. The factors are organized into causal relationships, and there are hierarchical relationships among the factors. (See Exhibit 7.1.)

This is not a process model; that is, it is not a manual or a how-to for implementing change. Rather, its power lies in the causal linkages, the "ripple" effect among variables. Used effectively, the model facilitates an understanding of why change is necessary in the client organization and in what specific areas that change must take place.

It is not a static model. The variables are constantly reconfigured and reconstructed by use on change engagements and by client-learning experiences and insights. Change can originate in one or more of the variables. However, the higher in the hierarchy a variable is (e.g., leadership, mission, and strategy), the greater the influence it will have on changes in other variables.

The elements belong to two categories: the transformational and the transactional. Both types are necessary for successful change management. The transformational elements are concerned primarily with the change itself—that is, with the

Exhibit 7.1

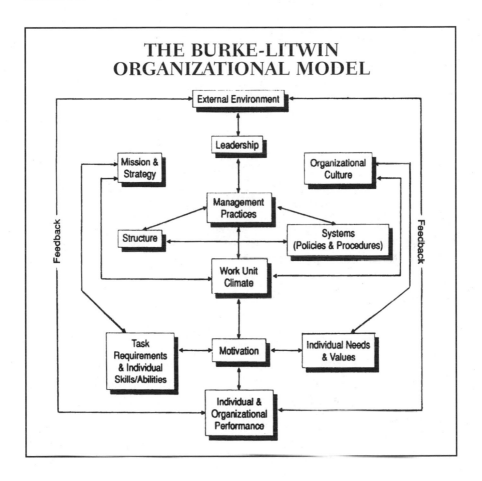

communication of a vision of the future. These transformational elements are usually associated with corporate *leadership:* having a vision, creating ideas, providing inspiration, developing long-range plans and goals, and behaving in an intuitive, empathic way.

The transactional elements focus primarily on the process of change—that is, agreeing on expectations (as well as a system of rewards and sanctions for degrees of compliance with the expectations). These transactional elements are usually associated with *management*: creating motivation, involvement, commitment; identifying and solving problems; creating short-range plans and goals consistent with the long-range transformational ones.

The Burke-Litwin model attempts to "distinguish between the set of variables that influence and are influenced by climate and those influenced by culture. [They] postulate two distinct sets of organizational dynamics, one primarily associated with the transactional level of human behavior—the everyday interactions and exchanges that more directly create climate conditions. The second set of dynamics is concerned with processes of organizational transformation, that is, fundamental changes in behavior (e.g., value shifts). Such transformational processes are required for genuine change in the culture of an organization."[1]

The Burke-Litwin model can be used as an organizational framework.

THE ORGANIZATIONAL DESIGN MODEL

Another model sometimes used is organizational design. (See Exhibit 7.2.) It focuses on critical elements in managing complex change. Beyond assessing customer needs and expectations and the best strategy to reflect them, it concentrates primarily on key business processes—in other words, on how work is done—and how they will affect the entire change process. Success will then depend on the degree of commitment change sponsors can obtain from employees.

In order to prepare the ground for optimum results, assessment must be both qualitative and quantitative in nature. Qualitative research, done through personal interviews and focus groups, offers an opportunity to probe for attitudes and listen for concerns and issues. It helps to identify the current culture and to measure the gap between it and the desired orga-

1. W. Warner Burke and George H. Litwin, "A Causal Model of Organizational Performance and Change," *Journal of Management* (Vol. 18, No. 3, 1992), pp. 523–545.

Exhibit 7.2

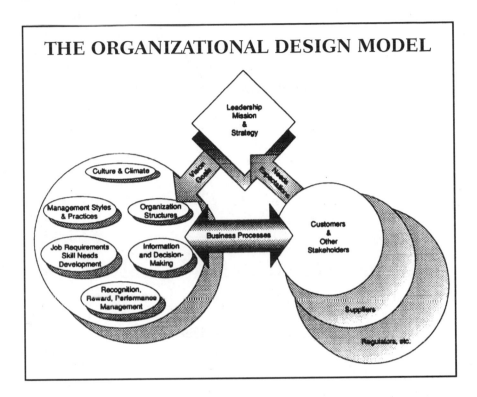

THE ORGANIZATIONAL DESIGN MODEL

nizational environment. Moreover, it provides comprehensive input for a quantitative study or quantitative assessment, based on surveys that track and monitor attitudes and processes.

Making comparisons is another useful approach. The first comparison an organization may wish to make is between its survey results and those of similar organizations or employee groups. For example, a manufacturing company may compare itself to all other manufacturers, or its managers to all other manufacturing managers. A government agency may compare its results to all other public or private sector organizations that do similar work, or its clerical employees to all other government clerical workers. These are meaningful comparisons. They show whether an organization or its subunits are above or below average within a specified classification. They can lead to improvement action, particularly if an organization is below average for one or more factors. But these comparisons are not benchmarks, because "average" is not "best."

A change management cultural assessment benchmark would be the results of the "best" organizations represented in the database. For example, the highest score of any organization for a factor such as "readiness to accept change" could become the benchmark of an organization that wanted to improve this factor. However, being "best" in financial and competitive performance does not always mean that a company has the most desirable culture or that it is open to the required changes.[2] Whatever the results, they can be used to formalize business strategies.

THE PLANNING PHASE

- What is the desired future state of the organization to be brought about by the change project? Where is the organization now, relative to that vision? What are the strategies for achieving the vision?
- What are the roadblocks to successful accomplishment of the change project?
- What are the desired objectives and goals of the change project?
- What is the impact of the change project on employees?
- What are the organizational redesign requirements to support the business process change?

The key objectives of this phase are putting in place the plan for implementing the change, overcoming roadblocks or resis-

---

2. David Wilkerson and Jefferson Kellogg, "Quantifying the Soft Stuff: How to Select the Assessment Tool You Need," *Employment Relations Today* (Winter 1992/1993), pp. 413–424.

tance, identifying and assigning roles and responsibilities in the change process, and establishing clear means of measuring progress.

Ideally, the outcomes of this phase are redesigned work processes, matrix management, a new emphasis on cross-functional interactions, greater use of teams and teamwork, and a streamlined organization.

The most critical aspect of change management is the human factor. Questions and concerns about the intent of change will be raised by employees. An organization with a work force suspicious of management's motives can make the best planned change strategy fail; an informed, trained, and committed one can be a major factor in achieving success. The entire human resources of an organization can be turned into a change implementation tool, divided into change sponsors, change advocates, change agents, and change targets. While change sponsors, advocates, and agents are selected to play specific roles as the change process evolves, everyone who will be involved in the new structure is a change target, and in most organizations that means the entire work force. In fact, sponsors, advocates, and agents themselves are targets before their roles become more supportive.

SPONSORS

These typically include senior management—in other words, the leadership. Coopers & Lybrand consultants organize working sessions in which the organization's leaders learn about the drivers of successful change. This facilitated session results in a detailed Change Map that will guide and coordinate leadership actions at all levels of the organization to overcome resistance and win commitment throughout the duration of the change until the new structure is a comfortable, workable norm. If the leadership of an organization is not involved in the change process, chances for success decrease. The leaders are the driving force behind the change, as they alone can have both parts of a job: the "doing and the dreaming."[3] In the words of one executive at GTE, "Our old culture rewarded doers, but, frankly, had been rather disparaging about dreamers....We now believe that the ability to balance dreaming and doing is the hallmark of all great competitors."[4] The role of leaders is: to establish a vision for the compelling need for change if one does not currently exist; to articulate why the "as is" situation is detrimental to the organization; and to emphasize the core process, restructuring initiatives and the results the organization wants to achieve. In other words, sponsors develop a general statement of change purpose. Coopers & Lybrand consultants apply a wide range of processes for leadership development, training, teamworking, and cultural development to increase an organization's capacity to innovate and manage change successfully.

ADVOCATES

Selected from senior management teams and consultants, advocates are the allies of the leadership, with the specific task of deploying of the vision throughout the organization. Communication is vital during this point in the transition, because it is through proper dissemination of information that employees can be enrolled in the change process. Also, involving employees in the change process early on cuts short rumors and promotes openness. Coopers & Lybrand consultants achieve this dissemination by means of employee forums, tailoring the message to each specific employee group.

As advocates, Coopers & Lybrand consultants conduct a number of focus groups at each level across the client organization. Topics include identifying barriers to change, identifying fear of change, and identifying motivational factors associated with each group. Pinpointing themes is essential to appropriate communication regarding the change.

---

3. David P. Allen, "Dreaming and Doing: Reengineering GTE Telephone Operations," *Planning Review* (March/April 1993), p. 29.

4. Ibid.

AGENTS

The agents are instrumental in making the major decision of working through existing structures or creating new ones. If the current people in their current roles can manage transition tasks, and if time allows it, existing structures can be retained to a certain degree. Even if other risk factors indicate a low likelihood of success, a skilled change agent can increase the possibility that a project will succeed by devising strategies and tactics to positively influence sponsor commitment, target resistance, and measure the readiness of the organization's culture for the change.

TARGETS

"Realizing significant improvements in the quality of a product or service...is *hard, hard* work involving a serious amount of grunting and sweating and heavy lifting on the part of *all employees*. It will mean 'doing things better,' but it will also mean 'doing things differently'—which is to say, it will mean *change*."[5]

"All employees" here are the targets of change. The more clearly targets understand the rationale for the change and the more vested interest they have in the change, the more committed they will become. So the two aspects of reinforcing the positive behavior of targets at the implementing stage are (1) to train targets and (2) to support and reinforce their commitment.

Training should not be conducted in the form of complicated, mass events but be clearly formulated and specifying the principles underlying the change. Objectives should be enumerated and the results of the training evaluated.

Support and reinforced commitment should come from the targets' increased skills due to training and their increased

---

5. John Guaspari, "The Role of Human Resources in 'Selling' Quality Improvement to Employees," *Management Review* (March 1987), pp. 20–24.

control over their tasks through empowerment. Additionally, targets should be asked to *involve themselves* in the change process—consulting them is one way of achieving involvement—to see quick, visible benefits.

A FORMULA FOR SUCCESSFUL CHANGE

The success of the change depends on all players understanding their part and becoming committed to playing it well. (See Exhibits 7.3 and 7.4.) It is up to the leadership to create an environment that promotes the understanding and the implementation of change and reinforces appropriate behavior by providing proper training, by making the data user-friendly, by supporting and encouraging both innovation and empower-

Exhibit 7.3

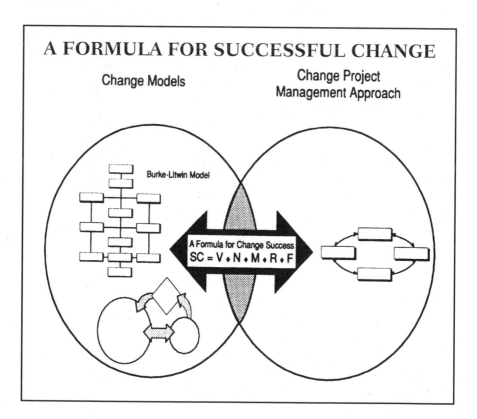

A FORMULA FOR SUCCESSFUL CHANGE

Change Models

Change Project Management Approach

Burke-Litwin Model

A Formula for Change Success
$$SC = V \cdot N \cdot M \cdot R \cdot F$$

Exhibit 7.4

ELEMENTS AND OUTCOMES OF DESIGNED CHANGE

ELEMENTS	OUTCOME
Accountability	Determination of specific roles, goals, and performance measures for the change
Adaptability	Strategy to learn from successful and unsuccessful change actions that are taken
Communication	Plan to influence all those who will sponsor, support, implement, or be affected by the change, including determination of a displacement plan
	Plan for ensuring that those affected by the change will participate fully in decisions and implementation
Focus, Purpose, and Vision	Mission statement and guiding principles for the change
	Specification of the results sought and criteria for evaluating progress and success
	Determination of the business processes which, when improved, will directly affect the change desired
Leadership	Plan for leadership actions to be taken through an infrastructure designed to promote and enable change
	Plan for dealing with and aligning the change with the existing culture, based on an assessment of its readiness to change
	Plan for the involvement of and teaming with bargaining units
Measurement and Results	Determination of data to be used to track implementation
	Determination of the measurable improvements to be achieved by the change
Momentum, Recognition, and Reward	Leadership plan for responding to shifts in the pace of implementation of change actions or acceptance
	Plan to reinforce individuals and groups achieving results consistent with the change with both financial and other rewards and to sanction those who do not
Skill Development	Plan to provide training to prepare for and enable effective participation in the change at all levels
Team Orientation	Plan to use teams throughout the organization to manage

ment, and by setting specific measurements for goal achievement. That, in turn, leads to a well-programmed system of
incentives, rewards, and accountability.

Defining change strategy and plans means focusing on the
three aspects of the organization: the matrix, the functional
aspect, and the product or service.

- *The matrix,* or main structure of the organization, involves
  its shape in terms of hierarchy (who reports to whom, how
  many layers of management exist) and in terms of the main
  purpose of the organization. In the case of conglomerates,
  this last point sometimes becomes difficult to define. In
  reaching out too widely, a company may lose its focus. In
  some cases, though, the broad scope that raises eyebrows
  on Wall Street may serve an ultimate purpose. When Reg
  Jones, former CEO of General Electric, spent $2.3 billion
  to buy the coal- and mineral-rich Utah International, Inc.,
  he had no intention of converting General Electric into a
  natural resources company, but wanted to commit the company to change.[6]

- *The functional aspect* involves the organizational operations,
  the processes through which products or services go from
  inception to customer. Managing the interface between the
  change process and existing operations is a critical aspect of
  change management.

- *The product* or service is the end result of research, development, design, manufacturing, and marketing.

By analyzing numerous change cases over the years,
Coopers & Lybrand has seen common themes emerge that differentiate successful from failed change efforts. The following
formula illustrates the critical success factors for overcoming
resistance to change:

6. Robert Slater, *The New GE: How Jack Welch Revived an American Institution*
(Homewood, Ill.: Business One Irwin, 1993).

$$SC = V + N + M + R + F$$

Successful change = vision + need + means

+ reward + feedback

Successful change will follow when:

V: A shared vision of the desired change has been developed, articulated, and communicated by the change leaders.

N: The compelling need for change has been developed and is shared by all employees.

M: The practical means to achieve the vision has been planned, designed, and implemented.

R: The reward systems of the organization have been aligned to identify and encourage appropriate behaviors compatible with the change vision.

F: Feedback is given at each stage of the process to monitor progress and provide information for continuous improvement.

THE IMPLEMENTATION PHASE

- Are desired behaviors rewarded and undesired behaviors proactively addressed?
- Does the performance management system support and reinforce the organizational change?
- Is the change being integrated into the overall organization? (For example, into work processes and training?)
- Does the organizational redesign activity fully support the change?
- What kind of feedback mechanisms are in place to collect data and measure the organization on the change project?

This phase focuses on strengthening commitment to the

change process by assisting individuals and teams in implementing the change plan. Special attention is paid to reward, recognition, and performance systems and to the degree to which teams and employees support the change effort. Special training is provided to those who will need it.

In the initial steps of plan implementation, Coopers & Lybrand takes an active role in ensuring that each step is executed properly. C&L consultants involve individuals and teams by the following means:

- *Changing the power and control structure.*   The leaner, flatter organization is more a set of core business processes than a pyramid of departments and functions. Identifying the core business processes and the role of individual and team players occurs in the implement phase.

- *Establishing feedback and performance measurement systems.* Without timely, regular feedback, the performance indicators cannot guide decisions or reinforce positive behavior. One task for change agents is to ensure that performance measurement systems like benchmarking occur at regular intervals and that the information collected is used for making needed adjustments in the selected course of action or the strategy.

- *Changing compensation and reward systems.*   Performance measurements used by Coopers & Lybrand are not necessarily those used in traditional management of operations. They focus more on managing throughput (how work is done) and output (the results of work) than on managing inputs such as the amount of money budgeted for a task or work unit. Also, they tend to be limited to the internal factors a manager can control, such as efficiency and productivity.

- *Coaching the leaders as they model essential behaviors.*   It is important for the CEO and other top executives to be visibly supportive of the change effort and involved in it. Only if the leaders of the organization "walk the talk" will others understand the process and follow.

- *Conducting training seminars.* Obviously, lectures and canned material are not going to be sufficient to address the complex changes the work force of an organization goes through to realign itself with the new culture. Training material is customized according to the needs of the organization.

- *Identifying new areas and schemes for redeployment as the need arises.* As process improvement creates excess capacity due to increased productivity, fewer people are needed to do the work. The extra people must be redeployed or let go. Part of the implementation effort is to make layoffs and downsizing as painless as possible through good communication, early retirement alternatives, job counseling, and outplacement.

- *Working at involving the entire organization as plans are executed.* Ownership of and commitment to change are built through personal involvement. Where possible, opportunities should be identified to include in planning and taking action those who will be affected by the change.

THE RENEWAL PHASE

In this phase, the organization must be probed for its ability to capitalize on the opportunity to build organizational resilience. Experience shows that human problems derail change efforts far more often than technical or procedural problems. Empowering people by truly sharing both vision and change strategy with them and by acting on their feedback and suggestions is one way of protecting against that. Establishing monitoring processes and reassessment techniques is another essential aspect of this phase. Organizations often know they want to get somewhere, but how do they know when they get there? In other words, if the starting point and the trip are important, equally important is the destination. And if they know it when they get there, how can they avoid bouncing back into the old ways, or the old culture? Credible measurements for cultural alignment are surveys and other feedback mechanisms, also useful for process analysis.

A routine data collection process for the change project includes:

- Surveys
- Interviews
- Brainstorming
- Written reports
- Focus groups

Other measurements to be carried out throughout the change process are:

- Sponsor commitment over time, to ensure continued energy and momentum
- Agent skills, to ensure that implementation is carried out cost effectively
- Employee resilience and increasing ability to cope
- Organization's ability to deal with feedback
- Budget and time targets for the change

Change management plans obey the same law as any other plans—even the best ones come up against unanticipated problems. The bonus is that unexpected opportunities also emerge during implementation. To make the best of both negative setbacks and positive outcomes, the change management team should meet often, remain supportive of the plan, and regularly review progress or formal modifications. A onetime intervention is in most cases better than no intervention at all. But a close working relationship between the organization's management and the consultants, with feedback and employee surveys at regular intervals and frequent checking of the change map for readjustments, will increase the chance for success of organizational change.

TOOLS, TECHNIQUES, AND REMEDIAL WORK

Many organizations don't formally monitor the change process. They have an intuitive, anecdotal approach. Even in those cases where the process is monitored, the issue is whether the relevant measures and criteria for evaluating success are applied. Is it how people feel? Is it market share? CRAIG SCHNEIER, CONSULTANT

A patient comes in to see his doctor for the first time in many years. Complaint: chest pains. Treatment: immediate major surgical intervention to bypass the clogged arteries and prevent a possible life-threatening heart attack. But wait. Is that all the doctor can do? What about long-term preventive measures—lifestyle changes that would have forestalled this crisis in the first place but that can, even now, help give the patient good, healthy years ahead?

It should come as no surprise that organizations manage pain in much the same way individuals do. What are organizations, after all, but an assemblage of money, material, and *people?* Just as our patient with the coronary-waiting-to-happen tried to ignore the changes in his body for as long as possible, too many organizations operate on what one Coopers & Lybrand consultant calls the "dampening wave theory"— namely, if you let the waves of change knock you around a little bit, the laws of nature—the natural resistance in the atmosphere—will eventually dissipate the waves' force.

THE PAIN—AND THE COST— OF LOST OPPORTUNITY

"You can pay me now or you can pay me later," was the favorite expression of that mechanic on the old TV commercial who wanted to change our oil filter. Change management consultants have the same motto. What we mean, however, is slightly different.

We ask management to compare the pain of disruptive change to the pain of doing nothing—hoping the waves of change will crash all around you but somehow miss knocking you down. Make no mistake. Organizations pay a price when they live with leadership styles, management approaches, systems and processes, and values and culture that are inconsistent with organizational goals. Encumbered by the weight of old ways that no longer work, any organization will have a hard time becoming nimble and flexible, with the ability to turn on a dime to meet the changing needs of customers, employees, and stockholders. When an organization cannot meet changing needs, it suffers the pain of lost opportunities—that is, lost competitive advantage, lost market share, lost revenue, lost jobs (and the list goes on!).

Change that takes longer than expected can cause an organization to miss a window of opportunity, wiping out the need for the change in the first place. Higher than anticipated costs because of the additional time and attention required compound that failure. Finally, a sense of failure frequently permeates an organization ineffectively implementing change, resulting in low morale and, even more damaging, change-shy managers who now believe themselves incapable of implementing change. These are the costs of not managing change—the high costs that many organizations are unnecessarily paying.

We live in a highly specialized era. The wealth of information and options in every field makes it difficult, if not impossible, for one person to master many different skills. Executives who are good at managing their organizations— good enough to perceive the necessity for change—may not possess the necessary organizational development know-how needed to plan and implement that change. They may also not possess the people skills needed to establish good communication through their organization about the nature and the reason for the change. That is when consultants are brought in. Beyond organizational models and frameworks, Coopers & Lybrand consultants have developed change management tools and techniques that they customize according to client needs.

TOOLS

Determining how information will flow into an organization's existing improvement methods is essential. In order to achieve this, consultants need tools—specific instruments used to perform a task. Examples are the Myer-Briggs type indicator, the organizational assessment process (OAP), the consensus builder group decision support equipment, the culture climate survey, the baseline load factor, the making change manageable (MCM) process, and the focus group process.

BASELINE LOAD FACTOR

A situational analysis tool, the baseline load factor shows that the implementation phase of a change effort can be jeopardized if its sponsors, agents, and targets are experiencing work-related stress before the change is announced. It pinpoints the current level of stress on the targets of a specific change project and provides early warning for potential stress-related problems and possible implementation failure.

CULTURE CLIMATE SURVEY

The culture climate survey (CSS) measures the readiness of an organization for change and the likely cultural resistance factors that might inhibit full achievement of specific change objectives. It is most useful at the assessment stage, but consultant entry into a client change situation will not always fall neatly into the beginning of the change cycle. The survey provides baseline and benchmark capability around such critical dimensions as organizational communication, job satisfaction and commitment, employee involvement, and work group productivity. (See Exhibits 8.1 and 8.2.)

Exhibit 8.1

ORGANIZATIONAL CULTURE ASSESSMENT

The Coopers & Lybrand Organizational Assessment Process (OAP) involves the use of the firm's proprietary Culture Climate Survey in conjunction with other assessment activities. The survey defines the key issues in each component of Coopers & Lybrand's Assess, Plan, Implement, Renew change management framework and points to appropriate tools, techniques, and interventions. The survey is used to determine how staff levels view elements of the current operating environment (i.e., communications, leadership, goals, decision making, change readiness, innovation). A survey-feedback-action planning methodology, the assessment process is designed to define in measurable terms the current culture and provide a baseline against which to measure the effectiveness of change efforts. It examines performance indicators and can create composite scores. For example, it scores organizations it surveys according to financial and competitive measures (e.g., annual reports, market share, and the like). Organizations usually want to see these types of performance indicators and how they may relate to cultural factors.

The OAP has been in use for more than 20 years and has been administered to 350,000 employees in 180 organizations. Its rich database makes it possible to benchmark the cultural data of the client organization against the norms in order to focus even more clearly on organizational strengths, weaknesses, and opportunities.

Exhibit 8.2

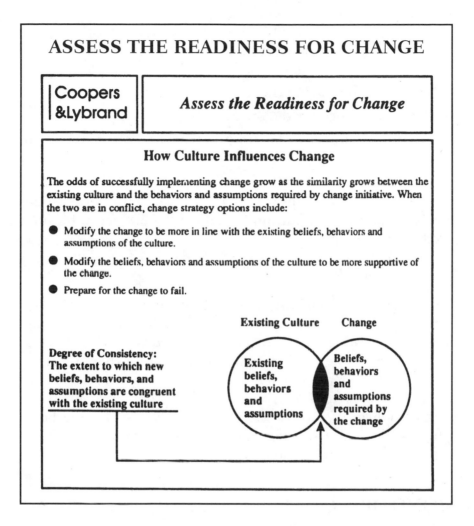

ASSESS THE READINESS FOR CHANGE

Coopers &Lybrand

Assess the Readiness for Change

How Culture Influences Change

The odds of successfully implementing change grow as the similarity grows between the existing culture and the behaviors and assumptions required by change initiative. When the two are in conflict, change strategy options include:

● Modify the change to be more in line with the existing beliefs, behaviors and assumptions of the culture.

● Modify the beliefs, behaviors and assumptions of the culture to be more supportive of the change.

● Prepare for the change to fail.

Existing Culture   Change

Degree of Consistency:
The extent to which new beliefs, behaviors, and assumptions are congruent with the existing culture

Existing beliefs, behaviors and assumptions

Beliefs, behaviors and assumptions required by the change

Other tools include the change project description form, the change resistance scale, and the communication planning process.

TECHNIQUES

A technique is a systematic procedure or approach that can involve the use of several tools—for example, change planning process, the organizational assessment process, and performance management system design.

For example, one technique integrates three basic dimensions of change in scoping out a client or potential client need:

1. Business issues facing the client
2. Phases of change for the business issues
3. Drivers of successful change that the client needs to address

The result is a snapshot of all the variables with which the client and consultant must deal for the project to be successful.

FOCUS GROUP PROCESS

A technique for collecting employee opinions and attitudes concerning the organization and their work, the focus group process is generally a more cost-effective way of gathering information on the organization and its culture than a formal survey or individual interviews. Focus groups are useful as an adjunct to other forms of data collection such as formal surveys or individual interviews because they can provide both information and a social response to that information that provides a "feel" for the organization.

MONITORING AND MANAGING THE CHANGE PROCESS

As change is introduced in the organization, incrementally or dramatically as the case may be, as business processes are redesigned and cultural values change, teams create a future organizational design that will optimize process performance. All key organizational design elements directly affect process performance. As they are redesigned, the new structure will drive the change in terms of the determination of skill needs, training, development, role/responsibilities definition, perfor-

mance measurement, compensation, incentives, job groupings, and management practices.

Organizational design elements in this important assessment include:

- Clarity and impact of organizational strategy
- Overall alignment of organizational operating and support
  functions
- Skill-needs determination, training, and development prac-
  tices
- Leadership and management styles and practices
- Job design, job grouping, and job enrichment practices
- Recognition, reward, appraisal, and performance manage-
  ment practices
- Information availability, decision making, and empower-
  ment practices

Results can be sustained, however, only if continuous
improvement is supported, and the "only [management] practice that's now constant is the practice of constantly accom-
modating to change."[1] Coopers & Lybrand can help the organization achieve continuous improvement as a norm in the
change-driven culture. The people who make the process work
are empowered with the ability to proactively reconfigure
process steps, systems, and organizational design to meet or
exceed customers' expectations.

MANAGING RISK

People in organizations will block a change in various ways
and for a variety of reasons. Yet the same people can be
encouraged to support the same change if it is structured differently. Understanding the risks and opportunities of change

---

1. William G. McGowan, interview: "Face-to-Face: MCI President Bill McGowan," *Inc.*
(August 1986), pp. 28–38.

is a vital step. Risks and opportunities are rarely self-evident from the start of a project but emerge progressively through the life cycle stages. Uncovering these factors requires continuous diagnosis and discussion among the various sponsors, agents, and targets of change. Using tried and tested survey tools allows deep issues to surface accurately.

As risks and opportunities become progressively clearer, change processes must be instituted to deal with them. The stages of the life cycle are never strictly sequential. New levels of data and awareness are progressively added and it is often necessary, for example, to revisit the goals of change in the light of experience during implementation. Coopers & Lybrand helps clients be flexible in responding to emerging needs without being distracted from the key business goals.

There is no prescription according to which precise change methods are used at every life cycle stage. Rather, experience and the insight provided by change models help determine a unique change map for every change situation. Critical issues, as we have seen in previous chapters, are:

- *Change communications.* When and how to announce a change is a difficult yet critical question. How the change will be perceived by the work force at the outset, how it will become clearer, and how knowledge of it should be cascaded through the management structure are some of the variables that almost always make this decision complex. Once conflicting factors are balanced, an optimal communications plan can be reached.

- *Change process.* The order of change processes is always critical. Experience shows that it is often desirable to bring some processes—for example, leadership and teamworking processes—as far forward as possible to overlap with the planning and assessment stages. However, this must be weighed carefully, along with other factors such as the requirements of the communication process.

- *Integrating technological and behavioral aspects into a single program plan.* This step is critical to ensure that the behavioral facts of life are not obscured by the technological dimension. We apply robust project control methods that deal effectively with both aspects, keeping them equally alive in the minds of change leaders.

REMEDIAL WORK

> I can't think of a time when we've gotten in early enough. We never, ever, get in at the beginning. You may go back to square one mentally, but there's no way you're taking the client back to square one. You have to find ways to squeeze the critical path of your own methodology within whatever constraints you've got.
>
> *James Clark, Coopers & Lybrand consultant*

Is there a bad time for consultants to enter a change process? Can it sometimes be too late? Coopers & Lybrand consultants' attitude is that they can enter a project and start to work on change issues on many levels. It's never too late to find solutions, though the problem, as always, is with people. One major client called in consultants when it was already in the third phase of a financial system design and implementation job and wanted to introduce change management because the next phase after detailed design was development and implementation. "[Management] knew from reading books that change management was a big issue, but they didn't understand what it was."[2] Using their assessment tools, the consultants asked the right people the right questions, from which all kinds of issues, such as misunderstanding the scope of the design or confusion on roles and responsibilities, emerged. Once problems became clear, solutions started appearing.

A DUAL-TRACK APPROACH

Organizational development experts find that a late commitment to change is due to "current pain." On the other hand, an early commitment is due to "anticipated pain." Both types

2. James Clark, consultant, Coopers & Lybrand, interview.

of commitments cause problems—in the first case because only short-term tactical action can be taken, and in the second because, although there is time, people feel less compelled to act. To treat both kinds of pain requires a dual-track approach. Sometimes these tracks run parallel to one another. Elsewhere in this book you will find a discussion of change management strategies that address anticipated pain by building the processes, systems, and other infrastructure necessary to support organizational resilience—the ability to absorb the force of recurring waves of change and bounce back quickly without getting knocked down.

What can you do when the flames are licking at your heels and resources like time, money, and people are limited? There are short-term tactics—corrective actions—that Coopers & Lybrand uses to remove barriers to change, such as lack of management commitment to and ownership of the change effort and outmoded policies and rules that stifle creativity and teamwork.

Of course, a dual-track approach is best. It treats the symptoms—the current pain—as well as the causes of anticipated pain. Says W. Warner Burke:

> We clearly have a set of standard tools that effectively address small- to medium-size problems in organizations today. A client says, "I am really having a tough time with my subordinates. I think I'll call our organizational development consultant for some team-building help." Another may say, "We are having difficulty with our customer service. We may be organized inappropriately. I think I'll call our I/O psychologist for some help." We have standard ways of facilitating teamwork and for looking at people's work responsibilities to see how they fit or do not fit together with other people's work responsibilities. We consulting psychologists and organizational development practitioners are beginning to face in another direction, not a direction that is incompatible with the place noted above, but different. We are on the threshold of a paradigm for the effective management of large-

scale organization change. We are beginning to understand much more clearly what the primary levers are for initiating and implementing organization change, levers such as culture, values, key leadership acts, the reward system, and management and executive practices.

THE TRIAGE SYSTEM

Coopers & Lybrand's four-step change management methodology—Assess, Plan, Implement, Renew—provides multiple entry points into the organizational change process. Change management can begin at any point. Organizations rarely sit down and press a button to start a change process. Much more frequently, a change project will have been under way for some time, perhaps with mixed results, and is now encountering problems of momentum or resistance.[3]

When changes in technology, processes, management approaches, or other solutions to organizational needs do not produce desired results, the change effort is often, in the language consultants like to use, "out of phase." To return to the medical metaphor for a moment, a consultant from Coopers & Lybrand applies what he terms "clinical pathology." "You have to find ways to squeeze in the critical corrective steps given whatever constraints you're up against. And those steps don't resemble the steps you would take if you were going into planned, elective surgery."[4] Triage is frequently called for to determine which steps are appropriate to treat the problem, which is often simply that the organization's people have not been aligned with the change.

This presents significant difficulties, especially if the organization has committed substantial resources (whether measured by dollars or man-hours invested) to progress well into the detailed design phase and is about to embark on develop-

3. Coopers & Lybrand, *Change Management—A Guide for Consultants* (New York: Coopers & Lybrand, 1994), p. T92311.IV–3.

4. Gilbert Betz, Coopers & Lybrand, interview.

ment and implementation. One Coopers & Lybrand consultant told his client, "I know you measure progress on this project by what you see. If you see a system being built, you consider that successful. But that's not a very good measure of success. You can build a great system, but if nobody is going to buy into it, it doesn't matter. Sometimes the fastest way to go forward is to stop. If you keep pressing forward and the people who need to buy in are not on board, you're setting yourself up for failure."[5]

THE AWAKENING

A consultant who has worked extensively with General Electric describes his experience: "Waking up the organization to the need for change is the most emotionally wrenching and terrifying aspect of a revolution. The protagonists have to shake up the status quo enough to release the emotional energy for the revolution. It is a two-step process. Step one is to kick-start the revolution. Begin by carefully articulating why change is necessary, and make certain that the top leadership team is in agreement. Step two is to deal with resistance. Expect to meet it in all key areas. At General Electric, there was technical resistance; organizational habits and inertia; political resistance, which involved leaders of different lines of business competing for limited resources; and cultural resistance, the resting-on-our-laurels syndrome."[6]

"GO FORTH AND DO GOOD"

For another company, "go forth and do good" was about as specific a phrase as the executive used on resource allocation. The senior management team wanted to redesign 20 or so of its systems, but each member of the management team had a

5. Kevin Walker, Coopers & Lybrand, interview.
6. Noel M. Tichy, "Revolutionize Your Company," *Fortune* (December 13, 1993), p. 115.

different understanding of the importance of each proposed change and how those changes would meet the company's objectives. One simple question kick-started the revolution at this company: "Why do you want to change?" It quickly became apparent that the executives were struggling with change because they had not set any single, compelling need that would serve as a beacon showing them the path to a new way of doing business.

The issue was whether these executives were prepared to meet the challenge of change. Were they going to be able to spend all the money necessary to redesign all the systems they had originally planned? Did they know how these changes could be integrated? Did they know what could be done for $1 million? For $20 million? What did they want their teams to accomplish? Did they realize the kinds of skills a team requires? What would happen if the teams came back with solutions the company couldn't afford? Were they ready to talk with their employees about change? (See Exhibit 8.3.)

A QUICK LITTLE EXPERIMENT

"Whenever an executive tells me his vision, whether he wants market dominance or increased market share, quality improvement, or a team-based organization," declares a consultant who works with major international businesses, "I ask him if I can do a quick little experiment. Let me run down the halls, up and down a few floors, and over to the next building and ask 10 to 15 people at random if they know what you have in mind and what they are going to have to do differently as a result of this new vision."

He goes to new product development. He goes to the loading dock. And he goes to places in between. After about 45 minutes, he has a pretty good idea of employee awareness. "My experience is that most people don't see the impact a change in vision, strategy, culture, or technology is going to have on them. When I talk with suppliers and customers, I get the same responses: 'We didn't even know they were up to

Exhibit 8.3

THE AGWAY EXPERIENCE

Here is a firsthand account of just such a confrontation meeting Coopers & Lybrand recently conducted:

> We got the key users of the redesigned business processes in a room to talk about the implications of what had been done and to find out what the gaps were in their understanding. We wanted to turn the key users into change agents, and they wanted to be change agents. But they couldn't be because they didn't understand what had been developed. We had to explain what the project was, what it wasn't, and what we understood the implications of the conceptual design to be, based on our understanding of their business.
>
> There were very dramatic gaps between what they understood had been done and what actually had been done. They had been operating under all kinds of false assumptions about inventory valuations and other things.
>
> There was a problem because the key users did not seem really engaged in the development of the new system. After that session, they became involved. That was the first time in eight weeks that the client had become engaged. We weren't near buy-in, but we had engagement. If change management had been introduced earlier, with the resources typically needed for success, this situation could have been avoided.

---

that. We've heard some vague comments, but we haven't seen any change and aren't sure what it will be, if any.'"[7]

Says a Coopers & Lybrand consultant, "If things are going to break down, they're going to break down in one or both of

---

7. Craig Schneier, interview.

Exhibit 8.3 (*Continued*)

The consultant who led this confrontation meeting stresses, "The lesson learned is it's never too late to fix a problem, but you've got to be really sophisticated, street smart, and risk-oriented to know how to push the right buttons to fix the problem."

As a result of the confrontation meeting, we were asked to help managers and human resources directors in a wide range of change issues, including project staffing, conflict resolution, human resources strategies, employee resistance, organizational communications, team-building, job descriptions and skill sets, performance appraisal procedures, and incentive plans.*

*Stacie L. Ratliff, "Change Management Is the Conscience of Agway," *The Change Leader* (July 1994), pp. 2–3.

---

two areas: leadership and communications. If change is not working, it's probably not very well supported. And it's not well supported because people don't understand what's required of them and what the change is, which results in large part from problems with leadership."[8]

HAPPY TEAMS AND VIGOROUS TEAMS

For more than 5000 years, managers have relied largely on intuition to assess the readiness of their employees to perform assigned responsibilities and to link an organization's culture to its outputs. In the absence of any systematic means to measure organizational culture, Egyptian managers classified pyramid workers with such labels as the "happy team" and the

---

8. Walker interview.

"vigorous team," reflecting the unique spirit displayed by different groups of workers.

Today managers have a wide assortment of social science tools, ranging from attitude surveys to in-depth cultural assessments. These help them align human resources capabilities with business objectives and overcome resistance to the necessary changes intended to realign the organization to the customer, economic, and environmental shifts in a particular industry.

The following measures can revitalize an existing, but stalled, organizational improvement effort:

Clarifying expectations. Before launching an assessment of an ongoing change effort, these three questions must be carefully answered in sequence. First, what are the anticipated results? Second, what must be measured? Third, what measurement indicators will be used? Exhibit 8.4 suggests which surveys are appropriate, depending on specific desired results, what is being measured, and the indicators used. The activities indicated in Exhibit 8.4 progress from the relatively easy at the top of the table to the fairly complex at the bottom.

Verifying the data. The usefulness of survey-based assessments is directly related to two factors: reliability and validity. Reliability refers to the level of assurance that the survey instrument does, in fact, consistently remeasure the same factors each time it is administered. Validity involves the level of trust a user has that the answers received do, in fact, accurately measure the factors the survey was designed to target.

Understanding the relationship between survey data and the organization's work flow. An effective survey must be capable of accurately targeting and measuring these organizational elements:

- *Input,* including commitment, job factors, organizational goals, job performance goals, work procedures, job training, and supplier quality.

Exhibit 8.4

MATCHING ANTICIPATED RESULTS AND SURVEY TYPES

Anticipated results	What is measured?	Indicators	Survey type
Head off conflict Increase morale Reduce turnover	Job satisfaction Areas of misunderstanding and mismanagement	Emotions and feelings Employee concerns and suggestions	Morale survey
Increase morale Reduce turnover Improve communications	Employees' perception of work environment Employee-manager relations Frustration levels	Attitudes Training Communications Working conditions	Attitude survey
Prepare organization for change	Internal environmental factors	Trust Openness Goal clarity	Climate survey
Understand the organization's norms, expectations, and values	Employees' reaction to organization's value system Adaptability/flexibility Strength of the culture How things get done	Rewards/risks Authority structure Intergroup relations Performance accountability	Cultural assessment

- *Process,* encompassing leadership, communications, planning, problem solving, teamwork, and coordination.
- *Output,* consisting of customer orientation, work unit performance, quality improvement, recognition, job satisfaction, and pride.

Matching the survey with organizational needs.   Attitude and morale surveys primarily identify symptoms of problems in the input and process elements and supply feedback on improvement activities. The climate survey gets at the causes of problems because it gives a fairly good view of what is going on in all three of the input, process, and output elements. A cultural assessment provides a more comprehensive diagnosis of an organization's readiness to undertake change because it studies the organization's underlying value systems.[9]

Organizations have a wealth of consulting and change management services to draw on when they wish their transition efforts to be accompanied by the least pain and disruption. However, it should not be assumed that however focused and comprehensive the approach, change will take place effortlessly or be a onetime process. An organization that wants to retain its competitive edge in today's global marketplace will integrate change and its management as a permanent component of its new culture.

---

9. Jefferson Kellogg and David Wilkerson, "Quantifying the Soft Stuff: How to Select the Assessment Tool You Need," *Employment Relations Today* (Winter 1992/1993), pp. 413–419.

AN OVERVIEW OF CHANGE MANAGEMENT HISTORY

The management of assets, including people, is a practice with a rich and interesting background. The idea of marshaling resources and organizing groups of individuals to achieve certain goals is evinced in the early annals of written history. In approximately 3000 B.C., the Sumerians developed a written language, which eventually became, among other things, a means of record keeping for business transactions conducted by temple priests. The building of the pyramids in Egypt required, besides exceptional engineering acumen, the management of thousands of workers. Even later, under the Roman Empire, the need for a well-run organization became obvious when Roman rule expanded to cover three continents. However, it was not until the early 1500s that the ideas of power and leadership received a thorough study by such writers as Machiavelli in his book *The Prince* and Baldassare Castiglione, author of *The Courtier*.

In the late 1800s, the transformation of England from an agrarian society into an economy based on power-driven machinery profoundly influenced managerial practice and philosophy. The onset of machinery brought with it, along with renewed economies, the tragic exploitation of workers. But early on in the Industrial Revolution, there were exceptions.

The management practices at the New Lanark factory are a prime example. Built in Scotland by Robert Owen, the business promoted a healthy and safe work environment. Robert Owen was a humanitarian as well as a shrewd businessperson. As such, he ensured that employees working in his factory lived in comfortable houses and received educational and training opportunities. He also put a cap on work hours, allaying any fears that the New Lanark factory would become a dangerous work environment like those prevalent throughout most of the country. Owens instituted an open-door policy; factory workers were allowed to approach management with work-related concerns and problems. The New Lanark factory's management style was progressive even by today's standards.

Although many of the factories constructed during the Industrial Revolution contrasted sharply in operating practices, they had one overriding similarity: controlling the work environment—in other words, the work force.

CONTROL AND THE SCIENTIFIC METHOD

By the late 1800s, the scientific method—the collection of data through observation and experiment and the formulation and testing of hypotheses—was becoming the established learning process in academic areas, especially in the United States. The scientific approach to learning gained acceptance in most professional circles, including the business community. As a result, the so-called Scientific School of Management evolved as an approach to organizational performance. Focusing on the design and execution of tasks, this school sought to optimize the productivity and efficiency of employees. It profoundly affected labor practices, with illustrious contributors, such as Frederick Winslow Taylor who established standardized production rates. Early critics disagreed with the assumption that there is a single, optimal method of performing a task. Furthermore, they believed that this approach generated morale problems among employees.

THE CLASSICAL SCHOOL

While the Scientific School was developed predominantly in the United States, a school of thought known as the Classical School began to form in Europe. Like the theoreticians of the Scientific School, those of the classical one were interested in increasing the performance of an organization. However, this school of thought did not focus on individual tasks. Instead, it focused on the organization as a whole. As a result, the Classical School was responsible for creating much of the jargon used in today's business world. Terms such as "chain of command" and "unity of command" were coined by Classical School authors. The military-like flavor of the literature published by the classicists was indicative of the way they viewed workers. Emotion was irrelevant. This sentiment is best exemplified by one of the school's most prominent figures, Max Weber, the German sociologist. Weber and other classicists extolled the virtues of a well-run bureaucracy. People became viewed as functions. Workers were expected to follow orders, and managers were expected to make decisions that enhanced the organization. Weber stated that the individual became "a single cog in an ever-moving mechanism which prescribes to him an essentially fixed route of march." In the movie *Modern Times,* Charlie Chaplin portrayed with poignant and comic accuracy just such an individual.

THE HUMAN RELATIONS SCHOOL

The dehumanizing element associated with the Scientific and Classical schools gave rise to a movement that sought to restore the human element in organizations. The leading thinkers of this movement were collectively known as the Human Relations School. Chester Barnard, one of its theorists, promoted the idea that organizations were not engineering products but cooperative entities. He stressed the principle of a natural social order within companies, formed through a natural process, not by a directive from top management. Barnard's work spawned several disciples. The book

Management and the Worker by Fritz Jones Roethlisberger and William J. Dickson was one of the first large-scale studies on productivity and the importance of social relationships in that productivity.

Fundamental questions discussed by proponents of the "Theory X" school of management—workers must follow orders or lose their jobs—and the "Theory Y" one—workers want to be self-fulfilled and therefore managers must focus on goal setting, professional development, and participative management—went on well into the period following World War II. Since the 1950s, new approaches have emerged, such as the Sociotechnical School, which is especially interested in group dynamics.

Almost every major school of management thought sees organizations as open systems affected by internal and external sources. An organization is made of departments, divisions, sections, and teams, which are interrelated and help transform inputs into profitable outputs. Existing schools of thought tend to focus on single, or several, components of this system.

Until recently, the principles of management have evolved relatively slowly. Now, in response to the demands placed on them by organizations' stakeholders and a changing environment, they have begun evolving more quickly. The contributing factors are complex, although we have seen that the three main areas generating the new differences are technological innovation, availability of information, and a globally competitive environment. With stakes as high as they are in today's business world, companies will undoubtedly continue to seek ways to change management practices in order to enhance company performance. Although new theories will form in the future, the past is a powerful reference in gaining an understanding of the complexity and strain of change and change management in organizations and their effect on the human being.

CHANGE MANAGEMENT

If the practice of management is as old as humanity, its formal establishment as an academic subject is a fairly recent one. (See Exhibit A.1.) Even more recent—dating back to the

Exhibit A.1

EARLY MANAGEMENT DEVELOPMENT

Year	Study
1910	Hugo Munsterberg applies psychology to worker management
1917	Meyer Bloomfield founds personnel management movement
1926	First public administration textbook contains a chapter on "Prestige and Morale"
1926	Elton Mayo writes that effective managers must understand a worker as a person with wants, motives, and personal goals
1930	Mary Follett's philosophy stresses individual motivation and group processes
1938	Chester Barnard posits that a leader's authority is based on the workers' acceptance of his or her communication
1947	Webert, Likert, and Argyris conduct research in human relations and applied psychology
1955	Simon, Leavitt, and Schlaifer emphasize human behavior in decision making and managerial psychology

1940s, when people became interested in finding ways to introduce organizational change without causing psychological and process disruptions—is the emergence of a new discipline, or mixed bag of disciplines, called *change management*.

In the past 50 years, as change in organizations and change management principles have become recognized, a number of management gurus have established themselves in the business community. The drastically changing environment, the magnitude of change, and the variables involved have proved fascinating to a number of people and institutions. In fact, change management gained recognition as far back as the 1940s. In 1958, Kurt Lewin, the social psychologist, broke down the change process into three stages: the known present, the transition, and the desired future.[1] The

---

1. Kurt Lewin, "Group Decision and Social Change," *Readings in Social Psychology,* ed. E. E. Maccoby, T. M. Newcomb, and E. L. Hartley (New York: Holt, Rinehart and Winston, 1958).

transition stage is described as painful, and unless it is well planned, the organization may not achieve the desired outcome.

Some 25 years ago came the birth of another discipline, called organizational development (OD). At first, what it meant to do was keep up with organizational growth, evolving into how change affects individuals and how individuals affect change. It is in fact the subject of change management, which is of profound interest to management scholars as well as to consultants who see organizational performance as the sum of individual performance. Rosabeth Moss Kanter, who is closely involved with studying change within the organization, writes:

> As world events disturb the smooth workings of corporate machines and threaten to overwhelm us...the number of change requirements go up, and companies must rely on more and more of their people to make decisions on matters for which a routine response may not exist. Thus, individuals actually need to count for more, because it is people within the organization who come up with new ideas, who develop creative responses, and who push for change before opportunities disappear or minor irritants turn into catastrophes. Innovations are designed not by machines but by people."[2]

For Kanter, not only is technical innovation not the answer to the challenges faced by many organizations; it can actually be "dysfunctional" unless accompanied by social and organizational innovations.

Considering that approximately one-third of adult life is spent in the workplace, management experts believe that involving workers in all phases in change within the organization increases the efficacy and acceptance of change. For change to be embraced across a corporation, communication has to flow. Many experts are engaged in analyzing the impor-

---

2. Rosabeth Moss Kanter, *The Change Masters: Innovation and Entrepreneurship in the American Corporation* (New York: Touchstone/Simon and Schuster, 1983), p. 18.

tance and the power of effective communication. This concept of effectively communicating the change to people was touched upon by Everett M. Rogers back in the early 1960s. His book, *Diffusion of Innovations*, describes the process by which change and innovation are incorporated into organizations. An overridingly important element in his book is the role of communication. Rogers completed a number of studies analyzing how new ideas and concepts were incorporated into organizations. His studies influenced many of the ideas on change today.

By the 1960s, organizations were viewed as open systems by almost every major school of management thought. An *open system* implies that an organization is somehow affected by internal and external sources. The various teams, departments, sections, and divisions are interrelated and help transform inputs into profitable outputs. Existing schools of thought tend to focus on single, or several, components of this system. Ralph H. Kilmann, consultant and a professor of business administration at the University of Pittsburgh, investigates "the intriguing possibility that organizational ego is, among other things, either an enabler of or a barrier to successful change. Can it be that organizations must first get their aggregate egos in order before embarking upon a program of nimbleness?"[3]

Although widely used by consultants and discussed by management gurus, change management has yet to evolve into a clearly definable discipline. The academic community treats the subject in a variety of fields ranging from psychology and behavioral science to organizational development to business administration. What management consultants witness, though, is that the weaving of expert theories is often done by people who have little practical experience and who have rarely confronted change management issues themselves. "What appears feasible in theory can fail in execution for rea-

---

3. CIO "Pain and Gains" (November 15, 1991).

sons that seem inexplicable unless the process is seen up close."[4]

Current management literature is full of articles on the "learning organization." Of interest are the contributions of Chris Argyris and Donald Schön (1978), who have said that "organizational learning involves the detection and correction of errors." Argyris and Schön differentiate between what they call "single loop" learning, in which members respond to changes in the internal and external environments in a way that allows them to maintain their current culture, and "double loop" learning, in which error is detected and corrected in ways that involve modification of an organization's underlying norms, policies, and objectives. This concept is comparable with the distinction between incremental and fundamental change.[5] According to Edgar Schein, for changes to occur, the organization must "unlearn" previous beliefs, be open to new inputs, and relearn new assumptions and behaviors.

In analyzing the consulting process, Everett M. Rogers and Floyd F. Shoemaker define the change agent as "a professional who influences innovation decisions in a direction deemed desirable by a change agency," while Garth Jones sees change agents as "helping professionals whose roles involve the stimulation, guidance, and stabilization of change in organizations...a 'helper,' 'mover,' 'doer.'"[6]

The factors contributing to change management practices today are complex. Present change differs from change in the past in three ways: technological innovation, availability of information, and a globally competitive environment. With

4. Ibid.

5. Richard Beckhard and Wendy Pritchard, *Changing the Essence: The Art of Creating and Leading Fundamental Change in Organizations* (San Francisco: Jossey-Bass, 1991).

6. Garth Jones, *Planned Organizational Change: A Study in Change Dynamics* (New York: Praeger, 1969).

stakes as high as they are in today's business world, companies will undoubtedly continue to seek ways to change management practices in order to enhance company performance. Most corporate managers know that the management of people is the greatest challenge facing them. Organizations and corporations, aware of the importance of this challenge, spend large sums of money both inside the organization and on outside consultants, to train, motivate, and empower the work force.

PERSPECTIVES ON CHANGE

"Tragedy is easy; comedy is difficult," an actor of long ago is said to have observed. In the world of change management, the principles are simple; the execution can be incredibly difficult. A Coopers & Lybrand consultant based in France joked, "Change is like spaghetti." His illustration is both clever and instructive. In an entity as complex and intricate as the modern organization, it is virtually impossible to manipulate one element without affecting another. As another Coopers & Lybrand consultant notes, "Process is the predicate of structure."

This book attempts to begin to unravel the strands of pasta. Academics and consultants have written volumes on the "etiquette" of this undertaking. But this book is equal parts theory and practical application. That vital second component—practical application—would have been missing without the magnificent cooperation of the organizations that graciously devoted their time to the development of this book. They brought life—tales of blood, sweat, and tears—to what would have otherwise been another academic prescription.

Because effective change management most often succeeds when it is a top-down initiative, we have gathered information from interviews with directors of change management efforts, chairmen and CEOs, firm managing directors, presidents, directors, and senior managers of human resources and education, federal agency administrators and section chiefs, local government executives, and last but not least, consultants inside and outside Coopers & Lybrand. We looked for "best practices," fresh examples that would illuminate change management do's and don'ts and innovative approaches to planning and implementing change.

In short, we probed for real-world experiences. Some were recalled with pride, others with pain. Our questions about handling the human aspects of change addressed these key issues:

- Formal, documented planning
- Success in achieving desired results
- Problems, both professional and personal
- Communications
- Change tactics
- Recommendations to other senior executives

All our interviewees generously shared lessons learned—sometimes expensively learned. Their willingness to do so strengthens our confidence in the future of change management. The scope of our inquiry ranged from federal and local government organizations to large and small businesses with domestic as well as global operations in a broad spectrum of industries. This representative sampling is provided as an indicator of the breadth of our survey:

Government
- A large federal civilian agency
- A local corrections division

Health Care
- A 600-bed acute-care hospital

Financial Services
- Insurance marketing
- Investment banking
- Retail banking

Manufacturing

- Aerospace equipment and auto parts
- Air-conditioning and refrigeration units and parts
- Boat building
- Elevator manufacturing, sales, and service
- Steel producer
- Voice and data transmission equipment

Telecommunications

- Local exchange carrier
- Regional Bell company

Other Services

- Vehicle fleet management

Coopers & Lybrand has had the pleasure of performing consulting assignments for some of these organizations. We express our sincere appreciation to all of them. Now we let these change sponsors and change agents speak for themselves. Hear them bear witness. What follows are candid comments—perspectives on change management from the many people who generously talked with us about their experiences. Listen, then, to the voices of change.

ON PLANNING TO HELP EMPLOYEES, CUSTOMERS, AND SUPPLIERS ADJUST TO CHANGE

Planning is important and necessary. It's just not sufficient. Some organizations spend more time planning than executing and have gorgeous, elegant plans but fall down in the execution. Executives are not typically held accountable for making change a reality. A lot is written and talked about, but far less is done. We want to make sure we get the resources to make it happen. We're not very impressed with planning for change. What's impressive to us is the execution of change.[1]

1. Craig Schneier, consultant, Craig Eric Schneier Associates, interview.

In the second year after we reached our vision, it took us almost a year to build a detailed implementation plan and do it in a way that everyone could understand what we were implementing, when we were implementing it, and how everybody would play in the game.[2]

Although we did take some steps to prepare for change, we did not start with a formal plan to address the human aspects of change. It would have been a great idea. Hindsight tells us that we should have done more to develop a plan first.[3]

The plan was fine for keeping managers focused on what we were doing, but it did not have a great deal of influence on people on the shop floor.[4]

2. David P. Allen, assistant vice president of benchmarking initiatives, GTE Telephone Operations, interview.

3. J. M. Shafer, administrator, Southwestern Power Administration, Department of Energy, interview.

4. Paul Hebert, former president, Corsair Marine, interview.

PLANNING TIPS

Make no little plans; they have no magic to stir men's blood.
DANIEL HUDSON BURNHAM*

- Dedicate sufficient resources to make change happen.
- Commit the time and attention of the executive team.
- Use graphics when possible; they're easier to understand than text.
- Remember the social factors necessary to support technical solutions.
- Build in time for management to understand the plan's who, what, why, when, and how.
- Specify how change will affect customers and suppliers.

*John Bartlett, *Familiar Quotations* (Boston, 1968), p. 810b.

At first, many of us were hesitant to get into the issue with clients because it meant talking about problems and inefficiencies in our operations. But initial contacts showed clients were sympathetic about problems. They also could see how some of our internal issues compromised the service they received, and they recognized that many of the problems actually originated with them and how they completed vehicle orders. They were enthused that we were proactively improving ourselves. Many of our clients became interested in applying reengineering approaches to themselves. Early skepticism from our account execs turned to enthusiasm as they saw communication strengthening client relationships, not harming them.[5]

Companies lay out a continuous improvement plan. It's a brief document. A lot of it is done with sketches that show what the shop floor will look like and what management systems will be needed to support that. It's got arrows like a flowchart. It's very effective because it's easier than text to understand.[6]

We started out with a set of assumptions on what it was we wanted to accomplish, a mission statement with a dozen characteristics of the new system—six of them technical and six of them social.[7]

ON SUCCESS IN ACHIEVING DESIRED RESULTS

We hope a high performance, highly productive organization that breaks down organizational barriers and encourages people to work together first will give us a significantly

---

5. Lynn Berberich, vice president for human resources, PHH Vehicle Management System, interview.

6. Mike Rother, consultant, Rother and Company, interview.

7. Marc Sternfeld, managing director, U.S. operations, Salomon Brothers Inc., interview.

improved organization that can respond quickly to business changes, and, second, a less costly organization.[8]

About one-third of the manufacturers I meet make significant change not only in shop floor technology or information flow or quality or workplace organization or cost or delivery or flexibility or reduced lead time, but also in how they manage—empowering people, moving decision making close to where the action is, getting away from command and control to what we call a "minibusiness" orientation where each department operates like a minibusiness. The second third make some technical changes and some adjustment in how they manage, but they still have one foot in more traditional management. The last third make very little change.[9]

In my own department (human resources), for example, I've noticed an enormous change in how people approach problems. Instead of waiting for someone else to fix a problem, they get together and form a team, identify a root cause, and develop ideas to alleviate the root cause. I can chronicle the change by what I hear at my door. People used to say, "I have a problem." Then they started to say, "I have an idea." Now they say, "Let me tell you what I just did to solve a problem." This does not occur in every case or in every corner of the organization, of course, but we're aiming to spread this attitude as widely as we can.[10]

From a business perspective, we want to go into underserved market segments. From an organizational perspective, we want to be a team-based organization, dynamic, fast to react, and customer-focused.[11]

---

8. Sternfeld interview.
9. Rother interview.
10. Berberich interview.
11. Doug Nelson, quality director, Prudential Direct, interview.

CHANGE IMPERATIVES

It is not the attainment of the goal that matters, it is the things that are met with by the way.   HAVELOCK ELLIS*

- Reduce costs.
- Increase market share.
- Improve cycle time.
- Boost quality.
- Sharpen customer focus.
- Gain flexibility.
- Restructure the organization.
- Empower employees.
- Introduce new products and services.
- Enhance productivity.
- Apply emerging technology.
- Redesign information flows.
- Enter new markets.
- Convert to team-based organization.
- Develop a shared vision.
- Achieve employee diversity.
- Strengthen communications capability.
- Develop employees.
- Redesign processes.
- Cut work force.

*Bartlett, p. 851a.

We wanted to develop a shared vision and decrease our budget. To me, the greatest indicator of our success is that I'm no longer the sole owner of the vision. The entire division is. In fact, I had very little input in this year's budget, and it was one of the most efficient budget processes we'd ever had. In the past four years, we cut our budget by 6 percent, and, yet, we've grown by 18 percent. For example, we've developed personnel efficiencies to such an extent that we spent $800,000 in designing and implementing a new program without requiring any additional budgetary expenditures.[12]

I always thought we were a successful organization, but I heard a lot of discontent. I was concerned that unless our people liked being here, we would eventually fail at our mission. When we started, I had three objectives in mind: to transform the working environment into one in which people felt valued and cared about; to help people become recognized for what they did; and, to help people feel they could contribute to our mission.[13]

ON PROBLEMS

The starting point is belief....It's critical that the chief officers of the company really believe in change, really believe they have to play an active and visible role. Even if they support change, it takes months to position what you're going to do in a way that they can articulate that message to employees.[14]

Most of us are pretty comfortable with the way we are, what we're doing, and how we operate. But today the typical organization is telling the middle manager that he has to be a different kind of manager. These middle managers have been promoted throughout their careers and gotten bonuses based on their performance, but now that's history. There is a natural resistance to change, a natural wariness, a legiti-

---

12. Tom Allison, director, Orange County Corrections Division, interview.
13. Shafer interview.
14. Allen interview.

mate cynicism that this is just another consultant, another boondoggle, another training program.[15]

This whole thing is really psychology. It's not really a technical problem. The higher you go in the company, the more people you find who have become successful by doing what they have always done. They have difficulty realizing the need to change habits. Another common problem is lack of a shared vision. If everyone is thinking about change in a slightly different way, it's very difficult to move the organization forward. You have to get the mental arrows lined up. Finally, there's lethargy. If you wait too long to do something, you may never do anything. But when people see change begin to happen—if some little thing is run up the flagpole and well received—then minds begin to change.[16]

People are resistant to change. One of the things people have the most difficulty with is when change affects their personal situation. Sometimes it's as simple as having to move their office. More resistance occurs when people don't have any influence on change.[17]

I think everybody who gets into this finds out the same thing. There is considerable resistance to change among the owners of the old processes. Our people are not devoid of intelligence. They've worked long and hard to get the processes to perform the way they do. Then a breakthrough team goes in. Breakthrough teams move very fast to get at root causes. They use radical objectives to reach breakthroughs. They seek outside sources of information—best practices and benchmarking—to fashion new ideas, new visions. When you walk in and tell the existing process owners, who are pretty hassled running the day-to-day business, that this breakthrough is achievable and you need them to

---

15. Schneier interview.
16. Rother interview.
17. Dan Stolle, director of human resources, Tellabs, interview.

join in an implementation plan and, frankly, take substantial risk by building the new instead of protecting the old, you just run into a lot of objections: "It won't work here." "You're benchmarking us against a different kind of company." "Our business is unique." There are a thousand reasons each of us might dream up to resist change. That's why we came to realize the importance of communications.[18]

About one-third of the work force was eager for the change and got on board enthusiastically. Another third initially dug in its heels but was gradually convinced reengineering was effective and it was in everyone's best interest to get involved. Another third still hasn't accepted the new ways of doing business. People moan, "We've always done things this way. We've tried things like this before, and they never work."[19]

The number one problem is people understanding and buying into the changes. There had been many management changes before I came along, but none had lasted. People looked at what I was trying to do with a jaundiced eye. The most difficult change was going from a top-down management style to one that was more team-based.[20]

I originally thought there would be resistance. But it's not resistance. Resistance implies a proactive conscious thing. It's more instinctive, especially when things get tight. When you have to make an instinctive decision and you're used to sitting in your own office and making all the decisions yourself, it's hard to remember you're part of a team and you're supposed to let others in on the process.[21]

The only person who likes change is a wet baby. The emotional aspect of change is a barrier. There is a tendency to

18. Allen interview.
19. Berberich interview.
20. Hebert interview.
21. Sternfeld interview.

take control, go back to the hierarchy of an authoritative regime. That kills the change process.[22]

I had my own career and a lot of my own ideas. The hardest thing to do is to be humble and leave behind preconceived ideas. To create a team, you've got to have enough humility to allow communication and other people's ideas to get explored and not shut them down.[23]

I have a client whose management team cringes when the CEO goes out jogging because when he's out running, he tends to think of all kinds of things that need to be changing. The CEO is out jogging, and his management team is inside praying for rain. If you're going to make change happen, you have to be open to new ideas, new information, and new processes. People are initially closed, or semi-closed, to new information and new approaches. It can be something very micro. Is a manager or an employee willing to listen to someone else's point of view? Is a manager willing to ask, "What do you think we should do? Do you have any ideas?" Are employees and others in the organization willing to listen to customers, suppliers, and peers?[24]

It's very difficult to try to get people who have dealt in a certain way with certain values for their whole lives to change all of a sudden. You can't stand up in front of 600 people in an auditorium and say, "By tomorrow, we're going to be different." It doesn't work. Culture change is big time. I don't expect it to happen in a year, but I have to make sure we keep moving in the right direction and look for signs, talk to people, see how they operate, watch their performance. Personally, the hardest thing for me is managing the transition, reengineering everything, changing everything, sustain-

22. Allison interview.
23. Allen interview.
24. Schneier interview.

PROBLEMS

Pain is short, and joy is eternal.
JOHANN CHRISTOPH FRIEDRICH VON SCHILLER, 1801*

- Lack of active, visible management
- Snapback to old ways, end runs that subvert new ways
- Inadequate measures to evaluate success; employees perceive measures as management's whip or way to justify downsizing
- Management's loss of power, employee empowerment
- Resistance from owners of old processes, middle management's wariness, cynicism
- Reluctance to explore new ideas, especially on management's part
- Moving from top-down to bottom-up management style
- Downsizing
- Organizational understanding of change; buying in
- Making change agents accountable
- Conflict for team members between functional and cross-functional responsibilities
- No change management leadership capability
- Hesitancy to engage in constructive confrontation and challenge old ways

ing the momentum of change, while still doing a good job running the business every day.[25]

If people who are not at a high enough level are brought into the change effort or if people are interested, committed,

---

25. Sternfeld interview.

(*Continued*)

- Cultural clash among organizational units, especially various global locations
- Track record of failed change initiatives
- Managing the transition from present state to desired state while still running the business
- Little top-down, bottom-up trust
- Restructuring the organization
- Developing a shared vision
- Organizational inertia

*Bartlett, p. 498b.

---

and supportive but not accountable, then we see the potential for problems.[26]

Typically in an organization, when an individual goes on a team, that responsibility goes on his plate, but nothing comes off his plate. There is always a conflict for a team member between his real functional job and his cross-functional team.[27]

Managers gasped when the initial reengineering team was selected and given full-time roles. They felt we had taken the best people out of their line roles and the organization would fall apart. Many tried to get their people back.[28]

26. Schneier interview.
27. Schneier interview.
28. Berberich interview.

The capability to lead change is critical and in short supply in most organizations. This is a key hindrance. Even if people conceptually or philosophically buy in, they don't necessarily have the capability to lead the change initiative.[29]

Many organizations don't formally monitor the change process. They have an intuitive, anecdotal approach. Even in those cases where the process is monitored, the issue is whether the relevant measures and criteria for evaluating success are applied. Is it how people feel? Is it market share?[30]

We don't deal with people's change in behavior. We don't change the levers like the rewards and measures that actually change behavior. All the time and money you invest to add value and responsiveness won't produce the desired results if you don't change the reward system or the performance measurement process. I've got a client that's looking at the procurement sourcing process. Quality and adding value to all the purchased materials is a big deal. Yet when I look at how the people in the procurement unit are evaluated and rewarded, it's on getting price reductions from suppliers. A big barrier is the inconsistency in our action and our work. We have to change the levers that we know impact people. A lot of people are analyzing barriers to change, but most of the time it falls to consultants, the human resources people, or some other internal staff to be the owners of change. The management team has to be the owner of change.[31]

We're all good rationalizers. The quality movement is an excellent example. Everybody thinks the quality movement is terrific and working great. Then you start to apply some measures to quality. You start to look beyond how many people were trained as a key measure. Organizations are thrilled

29. Schneier interview.
30. Schneier interview.
31. Schneier interview.

about their quality initiatives because they've committed an enormous investment of thousands of hours and hundreds of thousands of dollars to put 80 percent of the work force through two days of training. That's great, but can employees do anything differently? Where's productivity? Where's customer satisfaction? Organizations are patting themselves on the back for process, effort, and activity—not results.[32]

It's difficult to get senior management to fully appreciate what change means and to get them to model the new behaviors we want to see throughout the organization. And it's tough getting enough resources allocated to change management. This leads to the challenge of developing relevant metrics to show the value and worth of the change process.[33]

I have been here since 1962. It is very hard to see many of the people I know lose their jobs. The employees who are affected are, in many cases, people who are older, have been here the longest, and have shown a lot of loyalty. Weighing loyalty and hard work against the need to be very honest to the process has been difficult. I had to let people go knowing this would adversely affect morale. I knew many people would feel that senior management does not care about loyalty and hard work.[34]

We had to overcome upper management's lack of trust in employees and the employees' lack of trust in management. The management philosophy of our bureaucracy was "control equals power." Employee empowerment didn't fit that philosophy. Also, we had to adopt systems that identified and measured desired results, and employees saw measures as a means to cut jobs or punish people.[35]

32. Schneier interview.
33. Nelson interview.
34. G. Lee Griffin, chairman and CEO, Premier Bank, interview.
35. Shafer interview.

ON COMMUNICATIONS

At least half the organizations we deal with have not thought through the specifics of communicating to their constituencies what the change is and what's going to happen. There is often a lack of specificity in the communications plan about how information is going to get out or the consistency of the message. Most companies have some kind of a vision statement, but it doesn't always include desired results and the compelling business need and it's not always communicated effectively. The CEO or division president is often very actively involved in the change initiative, but the message often breaks down with the middle managers, line managers, and successive layers of supervisors. People understand they have to communicate, but often there is little consistency. For example, I have a client that wanted to make a change in several areas. The executive team was briefed and instructed to go out and talk to the employees. Documents were released, but it became evident that each member of the executive team interpreted the change a bit differently. Now there are a dozen visions of the change and different vocabularies used in talking about what's going to happen. There is often ambiguity, inconsistency, or just a failure to communicate to all the involved parties.[36]

One of the things that can lead to openness and receptivity is the communications process, which I don't think we utilize enough. I'm always surprised how little people know about what is going on in their organization. There are often examples of successful change initiatives in organizations, but they are not broadly communicated. Change is the art of the possible. You have to let people know change is possible. It's not just communicating about what's been done but what the organization is trying to do, how it will impact employees, and what everyone's new role will be.[37]

36. Schneier interview.
37. Schneier interview.

I have a real strong bias toward face-to-face communication with your manager in a natural team setting or in an internal-external, customer-supplier-process operator team. Face-to-face verbal communication—when your boss tells you what's cooking—is the most powerful tool for the change initiative. But the manager has to be credible. Sometimes managers stand up in front of teams, and their body language, especially given the track record of the organization, communicates that they are delivering a standard, perfunctory message that nobody is buying. If the manager is authentic, or can be coached to be authentic, and really believes in the message, and if the manager has credibility, or can gain credibility, then he or she is the organization's most powerful communications tool—a tool that's definitely not utilized enough. That doesn't mean other communications vehicles aren't useful, but they should supplement, not replace, the manager.[38]

In wholesale reengineering, many opportunities exist for miscommunication. When we began communicating with the work force, people were concerned about their future. The rumor mill was very active. We responded in two ways. First, we tried to continue communicating openly and constructively. We let people know reengineering might affect their jobs and that there were no guarantees. But we also told them what they could do to put themselves in the best possible position, including getting actively involved in the reengineering process, buying into the concept, broadening their skills to be able to adapt to new opportunities, and learning about other areas of the company where they might want to use their talents.[39]

Our communications planning to date has been largely tactical, not strategic. It has been reactive, not proactive. A

---

38. Schneier interview.
39. Berberich interview.

LET'S TALK: COMMUNICATIONS GUIDELINES

Good, the more communicated, the more abundant grows.
JOHN MILTON, *PARADISE LOST*, 1667*

- Give each employee a copy of the vision and mission statements.
- Communicate in small, team-based meetings or one-on-one.
- Establish culture-based employee orientation.
- Conduct a communications audit to evaluate organizational communications' effectiveness.
- Let people know change is possible; publicize success stories, even small ones.
- Talk about change frequently and consistently; develop a "change vocabulary" and use it.
- Extend the reach of internal communications to customers and suppliers.
- Control rumors.

*Bartlett, p. 346a.

notable exception has been a new employee orientation program that we developed addressing cultural issues. It introduces people to how we want to operate. It shows them how they are going to be evaluated and rewarded. Everyone—old and new—goes through the program.[40]

I met with every employee for about two hours in a small group setting. We have 1500 people, and it took me about

40. Nelson interview.

six months, but I wanted everyone of them to hear from me personally what it was I wanted us to do and how I wanted us to be.[41]

We conducted a communications survey with outside help to identify our strengths and weaknesses. As a result of this survey, we formed a communications team to develop a set of recommendations to improve our communications. We needed a common language to talk about change.[42]

At present, there's less communication with suppliers, but companies do tend to sell change to customers. The customers see teams tracking their own quality and costs, and they love it.[43]

Communicating well was important. People who were laid off six years ago read about it first in the newspaper. We had to try to build a climate of trust. We told everyone, "About 125 of you are going to have jobs and 500 won't. We'll let you know in the next six weeks who's staying and who's going." We had conversations individually with each employee...about what was going to happen to him or her and why.[44]

Without a doubt, more than anything else the increasing boldness and skillfulness of our internal communications throughout the process of delivering the reengineered vision helped us create the environment for change.[45]

41. Allison interview.
42. Shafer interview.
43. Rother interview.
44. Sternfeld interview.
45. Allen interview.

ON CHANGE TACTICS

In our organization design, we dedicated a human resource specialist to each department. These HR specialists became part of that organization, attending its meetings, learning its needs and operations, and providing on-the-spot recommendations and guidance on HR issues. Their knowledge and proactivity were important in predicting resistance, identifying issues, and surfacing the HR implications of decisions relating to change.[46]

Leaders have to realize they don't do anything. They get others to do it. When leaders understand that and begin to act on that understanding, they will ask employees to find out what has to be done instead of telling them what to do. And that's inverting the power structure.[47]

The most helpful thing I did in introducing change was traveling to each regional location and explaining what we were doing and why we were doing it.[48]

We conducted a lot of employee focus groups and critical issues surveys. We found people felt inadequate in their team behavior. So, early on, we put together training on team-based behavior, but it was done in too short a time, and we should have created the circumstances where those we trained could use the tools they learned right away. Now we are working on leadership training to improve the skills of managers in leading teams. We pretty much understand how to operate teams with people who work in backroom operations and do repetitive tasks. It's a lot harder to use teams with people who primarily work with ideas, for example, marketing. You just can't pull a bunch of books off the

46. Berberich interview.
47. Allison interview.
48. Griffin interview.

shelf, "sheep-dip" people in the new way of operating, and say, "Go and sin no more." What helped us was a high level of top management support for change. They gave us the resources we needed for the change process.[49]

We've done a very good job in training our team members but less so in training our coaches. Coaches were left to the end. In retrospect, if I could do it differently, I would train the coaches first.[50]

Everyone is writing about vision statements. Management goes off-site to identify objectives and then communicates that to its people. But how do we achieve objectives? What does the organization have to look like? That's the real vision statement.[51]

The best companies set up a regular schedule to interact with teams in pilots every few weeks. We call these "minibusiness development meetings." You need a management group to guide the teams, to provide support in team-building capabilities, to monitor the process as a basis for future action, and to spotlight and reward team—not individual—progress.[52]

One thing that really helps people adjust to change is seeing what other companies are doing. People don't like to be told what to do, but when employees go to another organization and hear their counterparts say, "I didn't like this at first, but now I love it and here's why," that talks.[53]

We learned you have to take a completely new look at incentives, measures, and rewards to get high-performance processes as designed. That encourages people to participate

49. Nelson interview.
50. Sternfeld interview.
51. Rother interview.
52. Rother interview.
53. Rother interview.

CHANGE TACTICS

It is common sense to take a method and try it. If it fails, admit it frankly and try another. But above all, try something.
FRANKLIN DELANO ROOSEVELT, 1932*

- Develop a vision statement.
- Don't just talk the talk, walk the walk. Get executives out front and up front about what is changing and why.
- Emphasize team-building and other education programs. Train coaches before other team members.
- Institute regular, formal employee surveys, focus groups, and other feedback mechanisms to assess organizational leadership, decision making, customer service, etc.
- Build a change management infrastructure, including change sponsors, change agents, and change advocates.
- Redesign the process before the organization.
- Encourage and reward team—not individual—progress.
- Assign an HR specialist to each organizational unit to raise and help resolve people issues.
- Use live pilot sites. Learn from failure.

*Bartlett, p. 970b.

in a different way than they did in the old processes. That's one really good reason to have pilots. In the early stages of our pilot sites, we began to realize that because our people were dealing with real customers in a real work environment, it was very hard for them to relate to the performance of the new measures because their incentives were based on the old measures. Measures are probably the real key to gain enrollment, and you don't get anywhere unless the employees eventually get enrolled.[54]

54. Allen interview.

A healthy attitude toward piloting is a significant factor in making change happen. Try things and throw them out if they don't work. Everything can be revamped and tried again. We're not married to anything. That's important because the ideas we had four years ago did not all work. One of our values is an operational philosophy that considers failure to be a learning opportunity. That's part of piloting. When something is not working, we try to learn from it.[55]

When our teams began to consider major process changes, it occurred to them they were messing with organizational boundaries, and some functions would no longer exist. We did something kind of bold and different and told teams to forget the organization, act only on a process basis, take the O-word off the table. We wanted to go far enough down the road that we understood what we were doing with the process before we messed with the organization. After a year and a half's work, a parallel team was put together to look at the organization, describe in detail the roles of management and employees, rewrite all the job descriptions, and restructure the organization.[56]

ON RECOMMENDATIONS TO OTHER SENIOR EXECUTIVES

Change never ends. People get into trouble most often when they say, "We're going through this change for the next six months and then we'll be done." You have to encourage and foster the understanding that change is continuous. You have to involve people in the process, engage them at whatever point is appropriate. Change is part of the learning process. It's growth.[57]

---

55. Sternfeld interview.
56. Allen interview.
57. Stolle interview.

You have to understand corporate goals and what the proposed changes will attempt to accomplish, recognize the obligation to align your team to manage the changes, develop a specific plan, including task assignments and target dates, find an easy way to measure progress, and adopt a philosophy and practice of personal identification with and involvement in the change plan.[58]

Human resources needs to play a leadership role, be one of the drivers of change management. As a key interface with employees, HR has important opportunities to advocate change and raise and increase organization learning. And, in addition to building internal change management capabilities, you have to hire people with a proven ability to flourish in a changing environment. We now have a more change-ready work force. Some of us would have a hard time operating any other way.[59]

Train. Train. Train. People need to have a vision of what is to be, but it has to be presented in real life out on the shop floor. You've got to be out there presenting it, getting to know your workers, reinforcing what you said yesterday. That's how your workers gain confidence in you, the leader. And you have to be 100 percent behind the change you want to make.[60]

To have an effective, valid training program, senior management has to commit to leaving the change process inviolate from budget cuts. You can't put the pedal to the floor and then cut off the gas. If you do, you'll generate a lot of expectations that will not be met and that will create cynicism. You have to know what it will cost to do the change management process right, commit to do it right, and sustain the

58. John Gamba, vice president of corporate and human resources, Bell Atlantic, interview.

59. Berberich interview.

60. Hebert interview.

commitment through hard times. You're messing with people's hopes and desires and the way they work. Don't tease people with half-hearted efforts.[61]

Develop the ability to absorb, manage, and support failure. As people start doing things they've never done before, they will find answers and solutions that are not always going to work.[62]

Prepare people for change. Pay attention to the effects that changes, no matter how seemingly minor, will have on people.[63]

You cannot predict exactly what is going to happen, so you have to be very sensitive to people's reactions and make adjustments as you go forward. Be humble. It's okay for management to go to the shop floor and say, "We're learning as we go, just like you are." People on the shop floor are extremely perceptive. When a manager comes down and says, "We've found a new way to manage," the needle on the B.S. meter swings off the scale. A little humility on the part of management goes a long way. You have to pay attention to the unfolding of events. Too many companies march off on a predetermined path—right off the cliff without opening their eyes and looking right and left. If you go out where the action is, instead of sitting in the front office, and find out what people are really thinking, what's really happening, what's really going on, that will tell you what you need to do.[64]

Effective, compelling, personal communication and the alignment of your people, systems, and structure are most helpful in introducing change. And you have to make sure

---

61. Nelson interview.
62. Allison interview.
63. Jean Taylor, director of educational resources, Memorial Medical Center, interview.
64. Rother interview.

FREE ADVICE

It is a bad plan that admits no modification.   PUBLILIUS SYRUS*

- Look around and stay alert to employees' reaction to even the smallest change.
- Use face-to-face manager-employee communications to find out what's happening.
- Don't punish failure; don't accept retreat to old ways.
- Be prepared to modify your plan, performance measures, and reward system to guide and goad employees' behavior.
- Take easy victories—"low-hanging fruit"—first.
- Realize that change never ends.
- Secure top management's commitment to change.
- Align people with change.
- Understand change goals—and their implications.
- Get employees to identify personally with change; get them involved.
- Know the cost of change management, make the commitment, and sustain momentum—even when times get tough.
- Don't delay.
- Seek outside expert help.

*Bartlett, p. 126a.

---

executives apply sufficient time and other resources to the change initiative.[65]

Show people quickly why they need to get past the stack of work on their desks and take on the change initiative. Be

---

65. Schneier interview.

quick and simple. And don't be afraid of incremental change. It's not too hard to show quick results. You've heard of low-hanging fruit? Well the fruit is on the ground here.[66]

Get expert outside help at the beginning. We struggled for a year before we recognized we needed help. Don't overestimate the willingness of people to change. Even when people are unhappy in their present situation, they still fear the unknown and are slow to change. Focus on methods of measurement and analysis as much as on behavior. Be patient and realize there will be back sliding to the old ways. Support people who make mistakes trying to change, but let people know that its not acceptable to go back to the old ways.[67]

In managing change, there is no substitute for going out into the field, getting input from those affected by change, and sharing your ideas. Make it clear management is supporting the change. If managers make people believe they're serious, most people will make the shift. We didn't do enough of this at first, but we learned.[68]

You have to be very up front with employees that there will be job eliminations and that normal attrition will not handle everything. I probably should have emphasized that more than I did. It's important to look at change as being positive in the long term, but there is a price in the short term.[69]

I've gotten quite an education and now realize missions of this kind generally fail because there was not the complete commitment at the top in the first place. If you don't start off that way, you've got to find a way to achieve that no mat-

---

66. Clif Williams, chief, Office of Cost Management, Internal Revenue Service, interview.

67. Shafer interview.

68. Sam Feinberg, former Coopers & Lybrand project manager for Carrier Corporation and Otis Elevator Company, interview.

69. Griffin interview.

ter where you are in whatever phase of your work. That means a willingness to take the risk to come out in the open, saying why the change needs to be done, staying the course, and being consistent in all messages. Over time if employees hear this from the boss, and keep hearing it, they begin to understand how everything fits together. What makes these missions fail is when the message comes out from the middle on behalf of the bosses without ever really engaging the leadership. The leadership has to be seen living the change. At that point, employees gradually begin to come along. As people—the teams, in particular—got to know more and more about what was possible in achieving this breakthrough, they were able to reach deeper down inside themselves than we were ever able to imagine. Given an outside stimulus, they were really, truly driven to greatness. That's the spark in the change effort.[70]

If I could do anything over again, I would have done a better job in managing expectations. I did not disclose enough to my employees or internal clients that there were going to be plenty of potholes along the way. I painted a picture of a wonderful world without telling them it was going to be pretty ugly getting there, and, actually, you never get there. It's a goal. Change is hard to do. It takes time.[71]

The best leaders think far enough ahead to know there's an impending crisis somewhere out there. They want to know what they have to do to change course before it hits.[72]

70. Allen interview.

71. Sternfeld interview.

72. Schneier interview.

THE RANGE OF CHANGE: AN EARLY PROGRESS REPORT

THE CONFERENCE BOARD CHANGE MANAGEMENT SURVEY

In 1993, The Conference Board, one of the leading global business membership organizations and a forum for senior executives to exchange information on key management issues,[1] asked top management to comment on their success in planning and implementing change management activities. The survey comprises 80 U.S. firms, 60 from Europe, and 20 European branches of U.S. businesses. Half are in manufacturing, and half represent service industries. Of the executives polled, 90 percent hold the title of vice president, director, or manager. Two-thirds are in human resources, 20 percent work in planning and finance or economics, and the remainder come from quality, logistics, environmental, or public affairs.[2]

The resulting report, *Change Management: An Overview of Current Initiatives,* was published in early 1994.[3] It focuses on how these organizations are addressing six powerful drivers affecting most organizations today. Survey participants ranked these drivers in the following order of importance: increased competition, fluctuations in financial performance, information technology, global expansion, strategic alliances, and

---

1. Kathryn Troy, *Change Management: An Overview of Current Initiatives* (New York: The Conference Board, 1994), p. 2.

2. Ibid., p. 9.

3. Ibid., p. 2.

mergers and acquisitions. Interestingly, fewer than 10 percent of survey participants report they were actively involved in responding to *all* these drivers in the 1983 to 1987 period. From 1988 to 1993, however, that number jumped to 40 percent.[4]

Regional and Industry Differences and Similarities

In general, U.S.-based firms and all manufacturers started change management before European-based firms and all service industries,[5] but the latter group claims greater success, which may be due to lessons learned from the earlier mistakes of U.S. firms and manufacturers.[6] (See Exhibit C.1.)

A closer examination of the six drivers reveals these trends:

- *Increased competition.* Ninety percent of all respondents place a high priority on this issue. One-third were addressing competitiveness before 1988. Both manufacturing and service industries are now active in this area, with 80 percent of the European companies reporting that their initiatives began in the 1988 to 1993 period.

- *Fluctuations in financial performance.* Again, 90 percent give this a high priority. Twenty-five percent indicate activity in this area before 1988. Since 1988, 75 percent of the European-based firms and about two-thirds of the U.S.-based firms have started to deal with this issue.

- *Information technology.* Eighty percent consider emerging technology to be a high priority. Fifty percent report efforts to manage changing technology prior to 1988. Forty percent of U.S. firms and their European subsidiaries have become active in this area since 1988, compared to 25 percent of the European businesses.

---

4. Ibid., p. 7.
5. Ibid., p. 13.
6. Ibid., p. 15.

Exhibit C.1

CONTRASTS IN TIMING CHANGE MANAGEMENT AMONG U.S. AND EUROPEAN RESPONDENTS, 1994

	U.S. COMPANIES (N=80)	EUROPEAN UNITS OF U.S. COMPANIES (N=20)	EUROPEAN COMPANIES (N=66)
Dealing with a significant increase in competition			
1983–1987 only	16%	21%	7%
1988–1993 only	56	42	78
Both	27	37	14
Dealing with a major shift in the company/industry's financial performance			
1983–1987 only	11%	—	18%
1988–1993 only	66	78	73
Both	23	22	9
Introducing and adapting to new technologies			
1983–1987 only	19%	7%	24%
1988–1993 only	39	40	49
Both	42	53	27
Expanding the business to global markets			
1983–1987 only	28%	12%	28%
1988–1993 only	44	53	51
Both	28	35	21
Entering into a partnership or strategic alliance			
1983–1987 only	9%	9%	12%
1988–1993 only	78	82	79
Both	13	9	9
Entering into a merger/acquisition			
1983–1987 only	25%	27%	14%
1988–1993 only	42	40	59
Both	32	33	27

SOURCE: Kathryn Troy, The Conference Board. Reprinted with permission.

- *Global expansion.* Seventy percent view this as a high priority. Forty percent expanded their operations before 1988. Manufacturers have been more active than service companies, perhaps because the survey includes a large number of financial services firms that normally confine their operations to domestic markets. European businesses indicate greater success, probably as a result of their history of operating in a multilingual and multicultural environment. From 1983 to 1993, there was no appreciable difference between U.S. and European firms in the level of change management activity related to global expansion.

- *Strategic alliances.* Fifty percent believe this is a high priority. Fifteen percent formed partnerships or other strategic alliances from 1983 to 1987, compared to 50 percent in the 1988 to 1993 period. Again, manufacturers were more active than service providers, and European firms report greater success. The level of activity in forming strategic alliances remained steady for both European and U.S. firms throughout the 1983 to 1993 period.

- *Mergers and Acquisitions (M&A).* Fifty percent also think this is a high priority. As might be expected, 40 percent report activity in this area during the M&A craze of 1983 to 1987 with about one-third active since 1988. Again, manufacturers undertook M&A more often than service providers, and European firms indicate greater success than their U.S. counterparts. U.S. and European companies disclose no significant change in the level of M&A activity from 1983 to 1993.[7]

STRATEGIC OBJECTIVES

It is a common observation that businesses sometimes embark on a course of change without a clear vision of their destina-

---

7. Ibid., pp. 12–15.

Exhibit C.2

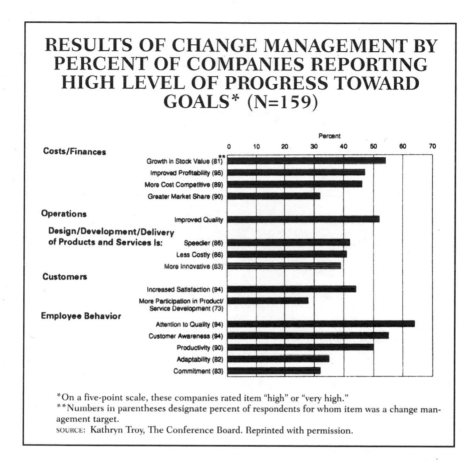

RESULTS OF CHANGE MANAGEMENT BY PERCENT OF COMPANIES REPORTING HIGH LEVEL OF PROGRESS TOWARD GOALS* (N=159)

*On a five-point scale, these companies rated item "high" or "very high."
**Numbers in parentheses designate percent of respondents for whom item was a change management target.
SOURCE: Kathryn Troy, The Conference Board. Reprinted with permission.

tion. How results-oriented are the executives polled for this survey? The Conference Board asked survey participants to identify those goals they were committed to for three years or longer and to assess progress realized. (See Exhibits C.2, C.3, and C.4.) Here are the outcomes expected and the perceived level of success in reaching those goals:[8]

8. Ibid., p. 39.

Exhibit C.3

RESULTS OF CHANGE MANAGEMENT— DEGREE OF PROGRESS BY INDUSTRY SECTOR

	ALL COMPANIES (N=160)		MANU- FACTURING (N=79)		SERVICE (N=81)	
	HIGH	LOW	HIGH	LOW	HIGH	LOW
Costs/finances						
Growth in stock value	53%	20%	48%	26%	59%	15%
Improve profitability	46	24	39	32	53	17
More cost competitive	46	10	57	7	39	13
Greater market share	31	23	29	22	34	23
Operations						
Improved quality	51%	6%	52%	1%	51%	10%
Design/development/delivery of products and services is:						
Speedier	42	15	45	14	38	16
Less costly	41	15	48	7	34	24
More innovative	39	16	38	19	41	13
Customers						
Increased satisfaction	45%	7%	45%	7%	45%	7%
More participation in product/ service development	28	23	27	15	30	31
Employee behavior						
Attention to quality	64%	6%	71%	3%	56%	10%
Customer awareness	55	6	57	3	53	9
Productivity	50	9	57	4	43	14
Adaptability	35	16	35	15	35	17
Commitment	33	19	32	21	33	16

Note: On a five-point scale, "high" refers to companies choosing "high" or "very high"; "low" refers to "low" or "very low." The difference between these two numbers and 100 percent is made up of companies choosing "moderate."

Exhibit C.4

RESULTS OF CHANGE MANAGEMENT—DEGREE OF PROGRESS BY COMPANY LOCATION

	U.S. COMPANIES (N=60)		EUROPEAN UNITS OF U.S. COMPANIES (N=20)		EUROPEAN COMPANIES (N=60)	
	HIGH	LOW	HIGH	LOW	HIGH	LOW
Costs/finances						
Growth in stock value	66%	12%	33%	33%	49%	22%
Improve profitability	58	16	37	32	39	30
More cost competitive	57	7	21	16	44	7
Greater market share	34	24	28	17	29	21
Operations						
Improved quality	55%	6%	42%	5%	50%	4%
Design/development/ delivery of products and services is:						
Speedier	46	13	53	6	37	2
Less costly	47	14	47	23	29	13
More innovative	48	18	28	11	36	14
Customers						
Increased satisfaction	44%	5%	40%	15%	42%	4%
More participation in product/service development	33	26	19	19	26	18
Employee behavior						
Attention to quality	71%	5%	53%	10%	60%	4%
Customer awareness	60	7	58	0	41	6
Productivity	52	10	47	6	50	6
Adaptability	41	19	41	6	28	9
Commitment	36	16	42	10	25	25

Note: On a five-point scale, "high" refers to companies choosing "high" or "very high"; "low" refers to "low" or "very low." The difference between these two numbers and 100 percent is made up of companies choosing "moderate."

SOURCE: Kathryn Troy, The Conference Board. Reprinted with permission.

- *Cost competitiveness.* Virtually all the executives point to increased cost competitiveness. About 50 percent indicate success in this area—with U.S. firms and manufacturers more than with European businesses and service industries.[9]

- *Customer focus.* Nearly all firms want a sharper focus on customers. Fifty-five percent are making progress in raising employee awareness; 45 percent believe customers are becoming more satisfied. There is little difference in the responses of manufacturers and service industries. U.S. companies and their European locations show greater progress than European firms do in emphasizing customer focus, but all groups are about the same in the area of actual customer satisfaction.[10]

- *Quality.* Again, almost all businesses indicate quality improvement is a target. Almost two-thirds think their employees are aware of this goal; about 50 percent see measurable progress. Only minor differences surface among all groups.

- *Profitability and stock value.* Approximately 80 percent of the respondents hope for a rise in stock value; again, about 50 percent saw the price of their stock climb, along with gains in profitability. Service industries have a better record than manufacturers and, with Europe in recession, U.S. firms are more likely to claim success in these areas than their European counterparts.[11]

- *Productivity.* About 50 percent report increases in productivity. Manufacturers perceive greater progress than service industries, but there is no appreciable difference between U.S.-based and European firms.[12]

- *New product/service introduction.* Approximately 40 percent say the design, development, and delivery of products

9. Ibid., p. 40.
10. Ibid., p. 41.
11. Ibid., p. 40.
12. Ibid., p. 42.

and services have become faster, less costly, or more innovative. Manufacturers and U.S. businesses show more progress than service industries and European companies.[13] When it comes to encouraging customer participation in new product/service development, however, 30 percent think they have been successful, with no great difference between manufacturers and service providers. U.S. firms show a slightly better record than European companies. Only 20 percent of the European branches of U.S. firms report success in this area.[14]

- *Market share.* One-third of the businesses attained increased market share. None of the groups surveyed took a lead in winning market share.[15]

- *Employee flexibility.* Winning employee commitment or achieving employee adaptability to change appears in the win column for one-third of the businesses. Fifteen percent to 20 percent say progress is slow.[16] Manufacturers and service industries show only minor differences in their responses, but U.S. firms and their European units outpace European companies.[17]

THE ROAD TO CHANGE

What change management initiatives are survey participants using to achieve their objectives? (See Exhibit C.5.) A majority of respondents list top-down changes in organization design, corporate strategy, work force size and composition, leadership style, and vision, values, and culture as areas of concentration. Approximately 40 percent view redesigning organizational structure, corporate strategies, and work force size and com-

---

13. Ibid., p. 40.
14. Ibid., p. 41.
15. Ibid., p. 40.
16. Ibid., p. 39.
17. Ibid., p. 42.

Exhibit C.5

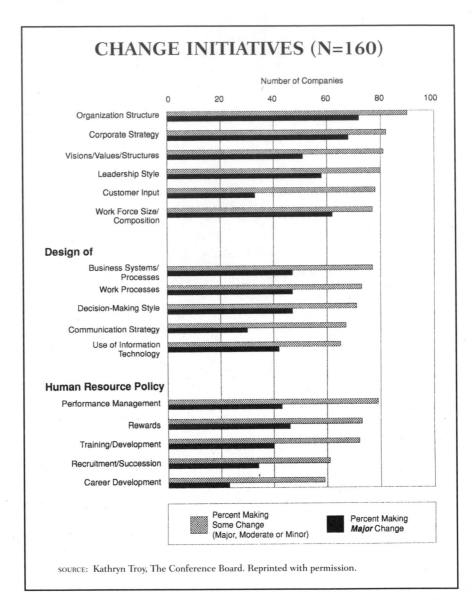

CHANGE INITIATIVES (N=160)

Number of Companies

SOURCE: Kathryn Troy, The Conference Board. Reprinted with permission.

position as successful. Executives are almost evenly split on whether efforts to modify leadership styles and decision making achieved desired results or just produced difficulties.

Similarly, changes in information technology, organizational communications, and human resources practices are considered to be neither notable successes nor problem areas. About one-third of the businesses made major changes in communications with their various constituencies, which is also termed a problem area by about one-third of all survey participants. Process reengineering was a success in about one-third of the cases and a problem about 25 percent of the time. Approximately one-third of the executives give a thumbs-up to shifts in vision, values, and culture; 40 percent rate culture change as troublesome.[18] Forty percent or more of these firms are decentralizing decision making and streamlining business systems and work processes. About 40 percent made significant shifts in such human resources issues as performance measurement and reward systems and training and development. And about 30 percent see major changes in communication strategies, the human resources issues of recruitment/succession management, and ways to strengthen relationships with customers and other constituencies.

IMPLEMENTATION: TIMING, COMMITMENT, AND SUCCESS

Survey participants commenced planned change management efforts throughout the 1983 to 1993 period studied by The Conference Board. (See Exhibit C.6.) The year 1989, however, emerged as the median date, which is also the year most respondents began to develop a new corporate strategy. In most cases, changes in organizational design, leadership styles, decision making, communications, and vision, values, and culture followed one year later.[19] The Board's report

18. Ibid., pp. 7–8.
19. Ibid., pp. 19–20.

Exhibit C.6

TIMING OF CHANGE MANAGEMENT INITIATIVES (N=160)

		TIME SPAN			
INITIATIVE	YEAR BEGUN (MEDIAN)	LESS THAN 2 YEARS	2–3 YEARS	4–7 YEARS	8 YEARS OR MORE
Business information technology	1988	25%	23%	36%	15%
Corporate strategy	1989	25	32	32	11
Leadership style	1990	34	26	29	11
Vision/values/culture	1990	34	30	27	9
Organization design	1990	36	29	29	6
Work process design	1990	50	32	14	4
Training/development	1990	37	27	19	17
Performance management	1990	38	25	27	10
Work force size/ composition	1990	38	28	22	12
Reward system	1990	39	20	30	10
Communication strategy	1990	39	32	21	8
Customer feedback	1990	46	24	23	6
Decision-making style	1990	41	32	19	8
System/process design	1991	57	19	18	6
Recruitment/succession management	1991	45	26	16	13
Career development	1991	53	17	19	12

SOURCE: Kathryn Troy, The Conference Board. Reprinted with permission.

investigates the timing, level of commitment, and perceived success or difficulty associated with these change management initiatives:

- *Organization design.* Ninety percent restructured their organizations. Seventy percent rate this a major change.

Fifty percent report a successful outcome. Two-thirds tackled restructuring after 1989. European-based companies report major changes and successful results more often than U.S. firms. Seventy percent of all respondents consider themselves global organizations, and 80 percent allow regional units some autonomy. Sixty percent say 50 percent of their change initiatives in this area had global implications; 30 percent believe 100 percent of their restructuring efforts were global.[20]

- *Corporate strategy.* Eighty percent committed significant resources to this area, but only two-thirds think their efforts were successful. Service providers were more active and claim greater success than manufacturers during the 1983 to 1993 period under consideration, perhaps because competitive pressures hit manufacturers before service providers and forced them to address this issue in the early 1980s. U.S. firms and their European units were more active than their European counterparts.[21]

- *Systems and processes.* Seventy-five percent undertook some systems and process reengineering; 50 percent consider this a major change. A majority of survey participants indicate activity after 1991; less than 25 percent were active before 1989. Less than one-third claim success; 25 percent see this as a problem area. Manufacturers are more active in reengineering than are service providers. There is little difference between U.S. and European firms.[22]

- *Customer focus.* Seventy-five percent employ focus groups, survey customers, work with or watch customers, or use other customer feedback mechanisms. Thirty percent say their efforts to improve customer relations were significant; manufacturers hold this view more often than service providers. Regarding level of commitment, there is little

20. Ibid., pp. 28–29.
21. Ibid., pp. 27–28.
22. Ibid., pp. 30–31.

variance between U.S. and European companies. Fifty percent focused on customer relations after 1991; 30 percent began customer relations activities in 1989 or earlier. Thirty percent of manufacturers, service providers, and U.S.-based and European businesses chalk this up as a success; 15 percent of the European units of U.S. firms achieved success.[23]

- *Work force size and composition.*   Downsizing and work force diversity were an issue for 75 percent of the firms; 60 percent say a major issue. Forty percent grappled with this matter after 1989; one-third took it on in 1989 or earlier. Manufacturers are more active than service providers; U.S. and European companies show about the same level of activity. For 40 percent, the results were successful; less than 20 percent disclose problems. Manufacturers and U.S. firms report greater success than service providers and European-based businesses.[24]

- *Human resources.*   Employee training and development and performance management and reward systems surfaced as an initiative for 70 percent of the respondents; 40 percent consider their efforts in these areas to have produced a major change. The level of activity was constant throughout the 1983 to 1993 period. Recruitment and succession management were issues for 60 percent of the companies; one-third made major changes. Most firms say these changes occurred after 1991; 30 percent were active before 1989. Again, 60 percent report dealing with career path and employee expectations for advancement; there were major changes for 25 percent of survey participants. Thirty percent of the businesses perceive some success in confronting any of these human resources issues, with U.S.-based companies indicating greater success than those in Europe. U.S. firms say they were more successful in achieving major

---

23. Ibid., p. 32.
24. Ibid., p. 33.

changes in reward systems, while European companies realized major changes more often in performance management. Service industries made major changes more frequently than manufacturers but were more successful only in performance management.[25]

- *Leadership style.*   Sixty percent of all the executives interviewed indicate major changes in leadership style. One-third say their efforts were successful with European-based companies, more likely to have undertaken changes in leadership style and more likely to claim success than U.S. companies. Forty percent of all companies initiated change in this area before 1989; one-third started after 1992. There is little difference in timing between manufacturing and service industries.[26]

- *Vision, values, and culture.*   This is a major area of concentration for slightly more than 50 percent of all businesses. And all businesses assign a high level of difficulty to culture change, although European-based firms and manufacturers report greater success than other groups.[27]

- *Decision making.*   Fifty percent made a major change. One-third count that change as successful; one-third consider it a problem. European firms and service providers were more active than U.S. firms and manufacturers and view the change as successful more often than other groups. Change in this area began before 1989 for 25 percent and after 1992 for 40 percent.[28]

- *Information technology.*   Forty percent made major changes, with service providers more active than manufacturers. Two-thirds made some change, and there was no appreciable difference in the level of activity throughout the 1983 to 1993 period. Twenty percent say the application of

25. Ibid., pp. 34–35, 38.
26. Ibid., p. 20.
27. Ibid., p. 23.
28. Ibid., pp. 20, 22.

emerging technology was a success; an equal number consider it a problem. U.S. firms and their European branches were more active in this area and report greater success than European companies.[29]

- *Communications.*   From 1983 to 1993 a moderate shift occurred for two-thirds of the survey participants; one-third experienced a far-reaching change. European units of U.S. companies believe their efforts constituted a major undertaking more often than European or U.S. firms. Service firms think they have been successful in this area more frequently than do manufacturers. Thirty percent focused on communications before 1989; 40 percent engaged in a communications fix or redesign after 1989.[30]

- *Monitoring progress.*   Forty percent measure their performance in a majority of the change initiatives discussed above. Specifically, one-third think they were successful in areas requiring a change in attitudes or behavior—leadership style, decision making, process reengineering, and vision, values, and culture. Another one-third, however, think these are problem areas—especially vision, values, and culture.[31]

CONCLUSIONS

In general, The Conference Board study suggests that survey participants are climbing a steep learning curve. (See Exhibit C.7.) Change management tools and techniques appear to be most effective in helping companies score gains in productivity, quality, and cost efficiencies. Success in other areas, like process reengineering and implementing new management systems and approaches to work (teams, for example), are hard-won.[32]

---

29. Ibid., p. 29.
30. Ibid., pp. 25–26.
31. Ibid., p. 38.
32. Ibid., p. 44.

Exhibit C.7

SUMMARY—SUCCESSES, DIFFICULTIES, AND EVALUATION EFFORTS (N=157)

INITIATIVE	SUCCESS	DIFFICULTY	PROGRESS HAS BEEN EVALUATED
Corporate strategy	58%	11%	56%
Organization design	48	17	45
Work force size/composition	41	19	48
Leadership style	33	31	44
Decision-making process	33	35	34
Work process design	33	28	43
Vision/values/culture	32	43	40
Constituent feedback	31	16	42
Performance management	28	16	42
Business system/processes	27	24	44
Reward system	27	19	42
Training	26	8	26
Information technology	20	21	35
Communication strategy	20	13	31
Recruitment/succession management	17	15	34
Career development	9	17	28

Note: The remaining companies indicated neither success nor difficulty.
SOURCE: Kathryn Troy, The Conference Board. Reprinted with permission.

COOPERS & LYBRAND 1994 SURVEY OF BEST PRACTICES OF IMPROVEMENT-DRIVEN ORGANIZATIONS

In the summer of 1994, Coopers & Lybrand, L.L.P., surveyed 272 U.S. and Canadian organizations to learn more about best-in-class quality practices. Best practice research, as this is called, analyzes the operations of organizations recognized as being top performers in particular areas. This survey focused on management methods for aligning and continuously improving business processes and infrastructure to support strategic market objectives. Here is a report on the initial analysis of the survey's change management findings.

METHODOLOGY

C&L researchers mailed a 68-question survey to executives and managers in charge of quality management in a purposive (nonrandom) sample of businesses and government agencies in the U.S. and Canada. These organizations were selected from several lists of successful businesses, government agencies, and hospitals.

The questions covered key practices in managing for improved quality, cycle time, innovation, technology use, and customer satisfaction. For most survey questions, respondents were asked to rate the extent to which they agreed that a specific practice was used in their organizations. For example, in responding to the statement, "Change leaders have a strong internal base of support," survey participants answered by marking a seven-point Lickert scale ranging from "Strongly Disagree" to "Strongly Agree."

OUTCOME MEASURES

Almost all the organizations surveyed had formal quality management initiatives in place. Eighty-three percent (N = 225) of surveyed organizations reported they had measurable results from these initiatives. This shows that we were largely successful in choosing a sample of organizations from which conclusions about "best practices" could be rightfully derived.

Those with results also rated higher their levels of success in satisfying customers, innovation, and use of leading-edge technology than did those who said they did not have measurable results, or did not know. The ratings were 13 percent higher for customer satisfaction, 20 percent higher for innovation, and 24 percent higher for technology.

RELATIONSHIP OF CHANGE MANAGEMENT PRINCIPLES TO SUCCESS IN INNOVATION

Change management is concerned mainly with the successful introduction of innovations into an organization. These innovations may include new technologies, new procedures, and/or new management approaches. Thus, one hypothesis of this study was that the more innovative the organization, the more it practices key change management principles.

Exhibit C.8 demonstrates that this is true for the most part. It shows 15 of the change management principles discussed in this book, each of which has a statistically significant relationship to innovation (at least $P = 0.01$, and in most cases, $P = 0.001$). The chart also shows the degree to which survey respondents agreed that their organizations practiced each principle. The bottom bar of the chart next to each principle shows the responses of survey participants who did not agree that their organizations had a reputation for innovation. The bars above the bottom one show the responses, in ascending order, of respondents who said they agreed their organizations had reputations for being slightly, moderately, or strongly innovative.

As seen in Exhibit C.8, innovative organizations appear to practice 14 of the 15 principles with more intensity than noninnovative organizations. The one exception is the principle "Employees understand the compelling need for change from the status quo," where there was less than a 1 percent difference between innovative and noninnovative organizations.

Strongly innovative organizations reported practicing 14 of the 15 principles with more intensity than moderately innovative organizations, and all 15 with more intensity than those rating themselves as slightly innovative. Moderately innovative organizations practiced 12 of the 15 principles more intensely than slightly innovative organizations, although often the difference was small.

From this analysis, we conclude that our hypothesis, "The more innovative the organization, the more it practices key

Exhibit C.8

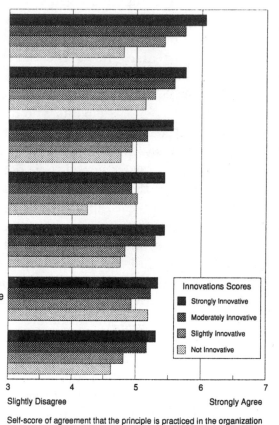

AGREEMENT WITH CHANGE MANAGEMENT PRINCIPLES BY SURVEY RESPONDENTS' SELF-SCORES OF THEIR ORGANIZATIONS' REPUTATION FOR INNOVATION

Change Management Principles

Change initiatives are driven by customer needs and expectations

Change leaders show consistent support for change initiatives

The visions and strategies for change are regularly communicated

Success with change is recognized and publicly reinforced

Organizational structures are aligned to reflect changes in management practice

Employees understand the compelling need for change from the status quo

Change leaders have a strong internal base of support

Innovations Scores

■ Strongly Innovative
▨ Moderately Innovative
▩ Slightly Innovative
▢ Not Innovative

3   4   5   6   7

Slightly Disagree   Strongly Agree

Self-score of agreement that the principle is practiced in the organization

Exhibit C.8 (*Continued*)

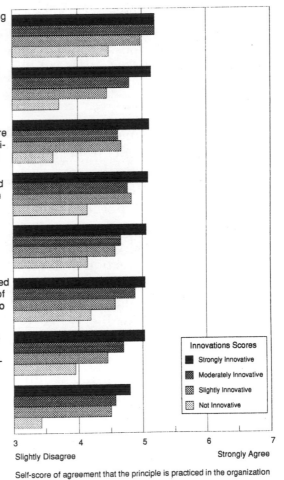

AGREEMENT WITH CHANGE MANAGEMENT PRINCIPLES BY SURVEY RESPONDENTS' SELF-SCORES OF THEIR ORGANIZATIONS' REPUTATION FOR INNOVATION

Change Management Principles

Responsibility for achieving the goals of change is assigned to a specific group or individual

Employees most affected by change understand what is required of them to support the change

Rewards and sanctions are used to support the organization's change initiatives

Changes are implemented at a pace the organization can assimilate

Success with change is recognized and publicly reinforced

Plans for change are based on realistic expectations of the organization's ability to change

The organization ensures that employees have the skills they need to accomplish change objectives

The progress of change initiatives is measured

Innovations Scores
- Strongly Innovative
- Moderately Innovative
- Slightly Innovative
- Not Innovative

3   4   5   6   7

Slightly Disagree   Strongly Agree

Self-score of agreement that the principle is practiced in the organization change management principles," is largely true. As noted throughout this book, success in innovation is more than a matter of technological breakthroughs. Such success also depends on an organization's ability to manage the changes brought about by innovation.

Finally, Exhibit C.8 shows that there is much room for improvement in managing change. For example, our preliminary analysis indicates that the principle "Changes are introduced at a pace the organization can assimilate" is one of the three major factors in predicting whether customers are satisfied with products or services. Yet, as can be seen in Exhibit C.8, even strongly innovative organizations score themselves at about a five out of a possible seven on this principle—just a little bit more than "slightly good" at following it.

LEADERSHIP

Among organizations with formal quality initiatives who reported measurable results from them, 47 percent of respondents said their vision was the greatest force behind these initiatives. Other driving forces were crises resulting from competitive pressures (24 percent) or crises from changing customer demands (15 percent).

Through a statistical technique called CHID (chi square automatic interactive detection system), the CEO's vision was found to be the strongest predictor of success in gaining measurable results from quality initiatives. These results were, in turn, the driving force for higher levels of customer satisfaction. Also, there was a statistically significant relationship ($P = 0.001$) between success in innovation and a CEO being responsible for motivating and leading an organization to improve its quality performance. Finally, according to the survey, when change leaders show consistent support for change initiatives, organizations are more likely to have higher success rates in innovation and the use of new technology ($P = 0.01$).

CONCLUSION

Some of the principles listed in Exhibit C.8 were among the variables in multiple regression analysis of causes in variation of success in achieving customer satisfaction, innovation, and leading-edge technology. Further study of the survey's findings will improve understanding of the relationship of change management to organizational success. But this much is clear from our initial analysis: *Change management does make a difference.*

So does leadership, according to our study. This should come as no surprise, of course, except in the degree to which excellent leadership apparently counts. This message needs no further study: *The CEO's vision makes a difference.*

C&L will be conducting further analysis of this survey over the next year. Interested parties should contact Coopers & Lybrand, L.L.P., Center of Excellence for Change Management, 1530 Wilson Boulevard, Arlington, Virginia 22209.

INDEX

ABOUT THE AUTHORS

DAVID K. CARR is the Partner-in-Charge of Coopers & Lybrand's Center of Excellence for Change Management in Washington, D.C., and the lead Partner in the firm's Change Management practice. His earlier books include *Best Practices in Reengineering* (McGraw-Hill).

KELVIN J. HARD is a partner in the Birmingham (United Kingdom) office of Coopers & Lybrand and is the leader of its UK Change Management Practice. He holds a Master of Arts degree from Cambridge University and a Master's in Business Management from The London Business School.

WILLIAM J. TRAHANT is the Partner-in-Charge of Coopers & Lybrand's U.S. Center of Excellence for Change Management. He is Chairperson of Coopers & Lybrand's International Change Management Group and holds an MPA from the American University in Washington, D.C.